BUDGET BLASTERS

First published 2002
Copyright Autocraft Publications

All rights reserved. No part of this publication may be reproduced or transmitted in any form or by any means, electronic or manual, including photocopying, recording or by any information storage or retrieval system, without prior permission in writing from the publisher.

The information is correct and complete to the best of our knowledge. Kit car building and its associated skills can be hazardous. The author and publisher accept no responsibility for any loss or injury resulting from any of the procedures or activities described.

ISBN 1-899814-22-1

Published by **Autocraft Publications, 1 Howard Road, Reigate, Surrey RH2 7JE. Tel: 01737 222030. Website: www.which-kit.com**

Editor: Peter Filby
Computer Graphics: Grapevine Design & Print
Page Design: Ian Stent
Printing: Grapevine Design & Print

CONTENTS

Introduction		5
Chapter 1	**WHY KIT CARS ARE EXPENSIVE** Reasons for kit cars becoming more expensive	7
Chapter 2	**KITS, KITS AND MORE KITS** The diverse range of kit cars outlined	11
Chapter 3	**CHOOSING THE RIGHT CAR** Deciding what sort of car you're after and how to find the right product	19
Chapter 4	**ANCILLARY EXPENDITURE** The things that can bump up your build cost	26
Chapter 5	**TRICKS OF THE TRADE** Where to make some handy savings	29
Chapter 6	**TIGER CAT**	34
Chapter 7	**BLACKJACK AVION**	41
Chapter 8	**MK INDY**	49
Chapter 9	**FISHER FURY SPYDER**	56
Chapter 10	**ROBIN HOOD**	63
COLOUR SECTION		65
Chapter 11	**JAS BUGGY**	88
Chapter 12	**LOCOST**	95
Chapter 13	**BANHAM X21**	103
Chapter 14	**TEMPEST**	112
Chapter 15	**SYLVA STRIKER**	119
Chapter 16	**THE OTHERS** Other cars which we feel can be built within our budget	129
Appendix A	**CONTACT DETAILS** Addresses etc of those cars featured within the main chapters	136
Appendix B	**SHOW DATES** The big kit car events of the year highlighted	137
Appendix C	**ACCESSORY LISTING** Useful contacts for a variety of different specialist suppliers	138
Appendix D	**CLUB LISTING** Contact details for clubs aimed at the budget builder	140
Index		143

Introduction

Have you got twenty-five grand to spare? I thought not. Well, that's the sort of figure you'd need if you wanted to build yourself a really pukka Cobra replica these days. How about £15,000 then? Still no luck? Well, what about £10,000...just about enough to scrape together a back-to-basics Caterham Classic?

If your bank manager would suffer a coronary at the very suggestion then fear not. *Budget Blasters* is here to show you that you can build an exciting and enjoyable kit car without resorting to a re-mortgage on the house. If you can cobble together £5000 (and in some cases considerably less) then we may have just what you're looking for, regardless of an industry that appears to be forever getting more and more expensive.

Indeed, despite a decade of ever increasing kit car standards (good news) and, as a result, escalating build costs (bad news), it appears that the industry is currently experiencing something of a backlash against the expensive, highly developed component car. While bargain specialist Robin Hood Engineering almost single-handedly waved the flag for budget kit cars during the Nineties, it's now been joined by a wave of newly developed products. These aren't aimed at the builder with a healthy bank account but rather the enthusiast with a few spare quid in his back pocket. Some of these cars are seriously cheap!

Perfect timing, then, for a book that tells you how to

Below: Kit car build costs have rocketed over the last ten years as standards improve. This lovely NG TC V8 is way out of our budget. Shame.

Above: Even Caterham's base model, the Caterham Classic is over £10,000 these days. Ouch! Thankfully for us, there are other options.

bag a bargain in a marketplace seemingly awash with out-of-reach exotica. The premise behind *Budget Blasters* is simple – find ten cars that can genuinely be built for under £5000. Have a look at the manufacturer behind the product, take a drive in the company demo car to see if it's any good and then talk to an existing owner who's actually gone out and built one – and here's the crunch – within our budget.

It sounds simple enough until you have a quick scan through the trade adverts in a typical issue of *Which Kit?* magazine. Initial prices can be promising, but then you often need to add VAT, donor components, trim, wheels and tyres, weather gear etc, etc and before you can say 'overdraft' we've raced past our self-imposed budget and are rapidly heading towards five figures – ouch!

However, there are a few obvious contenders which do fall into our price bracket, such as the aforementioned Robin Hood and the new gaggle of kits that come under the Locost banner. But what if you're not into the Lotus Seven inspired scene? Having collected together as varied a selection of cars as we can, *Budget Blasters* will hopefully show you that it doesn't matter what car you're after, it should be perfectly possible to build an example for under £5000.

Of course, choosing ten cars is just a neat number to work with,

Above: Robin Hood has almost single handedly fed the demand for back-to-basics kit packages. Sierra based 2B has been a huge success. See the company's latest model in Chapter 10.

and this book certainly doesn't suggest that these are the only cars which can be built within such a tight budget. Our final chapter outlines a few other options you might like to consider after you've read this book and hopefully decided that you can, after all, afford to build an exciting kit car.

Above: Fancy a traditional tourer but can't afford the associated prices? Well how about this terrific Tempest. Read all about it in Chapter 14.

But this book isn't just about highlighting ten potential candidates, we also hope to show you how to choose a kit car when you're on a tight budget, honestly assess your own skills when it comes to assembling it and give you a few insider tricks of the trade when it comes to sourcing components on the cheap. Above all else, we've tried to be realistic about our sums. £5000 is still a hefty figure to invest in a hobby, but it's a sum we feel will genuinely allow you to build a car you can be proud of.

Enjoy reading *Budget Blasters*, enjoy thinking about what may be your first foray into this exciting scene, enjoy building a kit car and, above all, enjoy saving some money along the way!

Chapter One

Why kit cars appear expensive

Flick through the pages of any monthly kit car magazine, add in a show visit for good measure, and the chances are you might well walk away, forgetting anything about building your dream car – build costs seem simply too high. Gleaming Cobra replicas, acres of leather in traditional tourers and supercar performance from humble Lotus Seven inspired replicas – none of it comes cheap.

But it wasn't always that way. Kit car building in the twenty-first century appears far removed from the bargain basement hobby that saw Eighties icons such as Dutton and Spartan reaching annual sales figures that would have today's manufacturers weeping into their fibreglass matting. Today it seems as though the no-frills, get on the road for next to nothing kit car has been long forgotten under a weight of independent rear suspension, leather interiors and composite monocoque chassis construction. The comparatively high tech industry that goes to make up the majority of today's kit car scene seems a far cry from its more humble scrapyard origins.

But before our glasses get completely rose-tinted about *the good old days*, let's not forget that those so-called halcyon years of the kit car are in many cases best forgotten. Quality was often worryingly absent from the manufacturing process while a quick MoT was all that was

Below: Kit cars may appear expensive today, but it wasn't always that way. Dutton Cars sold 1000s of kits at bargain basement prices during the Eighties.

Left: Blimey! No wonder kit cars are expensive when they look like this. Above: If kit prices are going up, second-hand production cars are dirt cheap.

needed to get a nailed together end product on the road. Is it any wonder that the kit car industry has struggled with a poor image over the last twenty years?

The drive for quality in the Nineties was therefore a perfectly natural progression if kit cars were to exist in an ever more stringently regulated motoring industry. Combined with the effect of a harsh recession, this was a decade that saw many of the old names go to the wall while newer, fancier, faster and more expensive offerings took their places. Develop or die was the watchword for those who came through this transitional period, Cortina donors being replaced with Sierra or, for those really going places, bespoke parts which were made to measure.

Of course, quality came at a price, and where the average kit car build cost might have been around £5000, it was soon rising to £7500 and now probably sits somewhere between £8000-12,000. What's more, all this has come at a time when production sports car prices have been tumbling. When Dutton was doing its stuff there was hardly a cabriolet in the country and the GTi was no more than a distant spec in VW's eye. Kit cars offered sports car performance for shopping trolley money. So what if the quality was lacking, where else could you find this sort of performance for the money? Today a second-hand Peugeot 205 GTi can be yours for £1500 and modern roadsters such as the MX5 are available for under £5000 – cheap kit cars are long gone. Or are they?

More recently a number of manufacturers have tried to redress the balance, led predominantly by the likes of Robin Hood Engineering and, more recently, the onset of the Locost phenomenon. And while the kit car press may have been slow to welcome these bargain basement offerings, it is absolutely clear that they've instigated a powerful backlash by enthusiasts against more expensive machinery.

Where a whole sector of potential kit car builders had previously been excluded from the kit car scene as a result of its increasing extravagance, now the floodgates are opening again. What's more, getting people into the kit car scene is simply vital for its continued wellbeing. Escalating kit costs have meant dwindling numbers of kit car sales over the last ten years and, while a handful of sales each year is fine for the manufacturer of ultra expensive replicas,

It's not all bad news, and the kit car industry is currently having a budget kit renaissance – largely fuelled by the massive success of cars like the Locost and Robin Hood (below).

it simply means fewer people get involved. And that means there are fewer enthusiasts to go on and build another kit car once they've finished their first one. Getting people on board, even on a tight budget, forms the bedrock for future sales further up the kit car ladder. But why have kit prices risen so significantly in the first place?

The fall in production car values

It's actually important not to get too carried away here. While there are genuine reasons why kit cars have become more expensive in recent years, there's also one big factor that makes these prices appear more expensive – the comparative affordability of mainstream alternatives. Where the equivalent of £5000 twenty years ago would have bought you a fairly mundane selection of second-hand offerings, today we're spoilt for choice.

Cheap performance was a big selling point then but today that same argument falls foul of some devilishly quick and entertaining mainstream offerings. The Renault 5 GT Turbo, Peugeot 205 GTi, Toyota MR2 and the iconic Golf GTi all handle well, go like stink and can be bought for peanuts. Even rag-tops are cheap, from an MX5 for £5000 or an MGF for £10,000 and even a Lotus Elise for £15,000. So perhaps it's not that kit cars have increased in cost over the years, but simply that the price of mainstream motoring has plummeted. Either way, £5000 buys a lot of car in the mainstream production car world. Conversely, initial impressions might suggest that you will struggle in the kit car scene.

Above: GTM may only sell fifty of these lovely Libras each year. That means fewer people getting on the kit car ladder which is bad news for the future of the industry. Volume production of cheaper kits is important in this respect.

Lots of budget kit car builders mean lots of people who will go on and build their second and third kit cars – good news.

Above: Kit cars will always be relatively high cost compared to production cars simply because of the labour-intensive way they are made.

Above: Homebuilt cars are getting cleverer and cleverer. This Dax Rush camber compensation suspension system is unique – but it comes at a cost.

But if mainstream cars have got cheaper, why hasn't the kit car scene kept pace? That's a simple one to answer because, while production car manufacturing techniques have allowed mainstream manufacturers to produce better products more cheaply, the kit car, by its very nature, remains a hand-built product, even at the manufacturing stage. As such, the manufacturing cost of a chassis has remained largely static over the last twenty years (discounting inflation). So while it may appear that costs have risen it may well be fairer to say that, by comparison, mainstream values have fallen.

Escalating kit car costs

Of course, to suggest that kit cars only appear expensive because those products around them have fallen in value isn't the whole story. The Dutton Phaeton that sold so well in the Eighties was a very basic creation, with a rudimentary chassis and suspension components transferred straight from a donor Escort. There's little doubt that standards and expectations have risen since then. Where some manufacturers would sell you a chassis without any suspension bracketry whatsoever, there aren't many of us who would entertain such a thing today.

What's more, chassis design has vastly improved since then, with more intricate designs that are considerably more rigid. More developed suspension systems have also imposed higher standards of production on suspension wishbones, uprights and the like, while manufacturers such as DJ Sportscars are even coming out with brand new, innovative suspension systems that are genuinely groundbreaking. The company's camber compensation system is completely unique for a road-going car...be it production or kit car.

If a basic kit package is said to consist of both a chassis and bodywork, then it's not just the metalwork that has improved over the years. Coloured gelcoat bodywork means enthusiasts can save on a separate paint job, but it also demands a very high quality mould from the manufacturer in order to produce smooth, blemish-free panels. And in the same way that chassis could be supplied without any bracketry in the old days, bodies were often dispatched from the factory untrimmed. That's to say, all the rough edges where the fibreglass matting curled over the edge of the mould were left on the panel for the builder to carefully cut off and file smooth. That's not something that any serious manufacturer would contemplate today.

So the quality of the basic chassis and body that come with most kit cars today is considerably more developed than it used to be. That means more man-hours spent by the manufacturer to produce a better quality product – all of which is great news. But someone has got to pay.

Not only is the standard of the basic kit package much improved, the same applies to the quality of the finishing items. A bucket seat and a roll of household carpet just won't do these days. The expectations of builders have a lot to answer for here. Allied to improvements in production car standards, so kit car customers are demanding a higher level of finish.

Manufacturers such as GTM Cars have developed the most intricate of interior trim kits that put to shame some of the offerings from production sports cars such as the Lotus Elise. Wonderfully developed, the GTM Libra's superb cockpit is a real treat but it comes at a hefty premium. What's more, it sets the standard for others to follow – if one manufacturer can produce something like that, then another will soon try and beat it. Which is all well and good if you have the money to indulge yourself but it's not so helpful when you've only limited funds but a passion to build your own car.

Regardless of cheaper production cars and improvements in kit quality, the reality for those of us with only limited funds is the same. Building a kit car on a budget is going to test your ingenuity and resolve but, as we hope to prove, it's far from impossible.

Chapter Two

Kits, kits and more kits

If you're a newcomer to the kit car scene then it can be a little bewildering deciding what style of car you like and, within that particular style, which specific kit you prefer. There are often several different examples of kit car within a particular niche, some expensive and some more affordable. However, certain styles of kit car tend to be more expensive than others. Here we try and outline the main sectors within the marketplace, their typical build costs and the specific items on a car that tend to inflate the end figure.

Cobra replicas

Typical build costs: £10,000-20,000
Prime contenders within our budget: None that we can think of without bending the rules!
Cost Escalators: V8 engines, Jaguar donors, large wheels and tyres, expensive paint, leather interior, extensive chrome brightwork, side exiting exhaust systems.

The Cobra replica scene is one of the largest within the kit car marketplace, and with good reason. These are spectacular looking cars, with big power, great noise, a comfortable interior and, most unusually for a kit car, considerable practicality. Closely replicating the fabulous styling of the 1960s AC Cobra, these cars tend to feature large V8 engines, full leather

Lots of expensive gauges for a fake snake, not to mention a complete carpet set, suitable wheel and expensive seats.

Above: Big problem with most Cobra replicas is that they need a V8 engine and, even in Rover V8-powered form, they're not cheap by the time you add in exhausts etc.

Below: One of the cheapest Cobra replicas is Fiero Factory's Euro 427, a Ford Sierra/Granada based car using the donor's 2.9-litre V6. Sadly, it's still too expensive for us.

Left: The Tiger Avon is the manufacturer's latest budget offering which can be assembled for well under £5000. Find out more in Chapter 7. Above: Originally based around the Locost chassis, the Stuart Taylor product has gone increasingly upmarket.

interiors and expensive paint jobs.

By and large they are not cheap cars to build but there are one or two companies producing cars that can perhaps be completed for under £10,000. These tend to feature four or six-cylinder engines taken from the Ford range of donors (Sierra or Granada). A gelcoat colour finish can help reduce costs while more basic interior trim eases the bank balance. However, we wouldn't consider that any of the current range of Cobra replica manufacturers could offer a product within out tight budget.

Lotus Seven inspired replicas

Typical build costs: £3500-£15,000
Prime contenders within our budget: MK Engineering, Stuart Taylor Motorsport, Tiger Racing, Robin Hood Engineering, BWE Locust, Formula 27, Sylva Autokits, Vindicator Cars.

Right: Unless using the complete Sierra rear suspension, IRS suspensions are more expensive than conventional live axled cars. Below: The Sylva Striker is just within our budget and is reviewed in Chapter 15.

Cost Escalators: Independent rear suspension, non-donor engine installations, paint.

Here's the big daddy in terms of the kit car scene. The Lotus Seven inspired replica marketplace is the most prolific in the industry, with well over ten different companies vying for your attention. What's more, these can be reasonably affordable projects and the cars' simple design and layout makes them ideal for the first time builder.

At its most basic, this marketplace has the Locost kit car, based on a book by Ron Champion called *Build Your Own Sports Car For As Little As £250*. While the book explains how to weld up your own chassis, a number of companies now offer pre-fabricated chassis to give you a head start. We've kept our estimate of typical build costs at a minimum of £3500, especially for those opting for a pre-fabricated chassis, but we've met those who've built cars

for considerably less (£1500), so it can certainly be done.

Kits in this niche tend to be marketed in one of two ways, either as a complete kit package requiring only donor parts to complete (such as a dead Ford Sierra) or those that are marketed as individual components (such as a chassis from £450). In such a highly competitive market you really need to do your homework here, since it may be that the more expensive but comprehensive kit package works out cheaper than sourcing all the components individually yourself.

The big news in this marketplace is the recent development of bike engine installations. Ultra-light in weight, developing lots of power and typically using a 6-speed sequential gearbox, these units can offer genuine supercar performance for seemingly very little money (say £1000 for the engine and its ancillaries). However, for our purposes there's little doubt that if you head this route you'll be stretching your budget.

Using a bike engine will have an impact on many other vital components for which the manufacturer may charge extra. These might include a lightweight chassis, bespoke gear linkage, special exhaust, new wiring loom, additional engine cradle, special propshaft and, if you want a reverse gear, a bespoke reverse gearbox in addition to the bike's standard six forward gears.

Indeed, opting for any engine other than the one that essentially came free with your donor car is going to have a significant impact on your budget.

However, the big advantage with this type of car is that you can get away with ultra-basic interior trimming, gelcoat colour body panels and sensibly sized wheels and tyres. A simple layout and diminutive size mean it will fit in your garage and be relatively easy to assemble.

And the best bit? Even a dirt cheap example can be made to handle beautifully – these really give you the biggest buzz for your bucks when it comes to driving adrenalin. Quite simply, the Lotus Seven inspired replica has to be a prime contender if you want to build a kit car within a tight budget.

Above: Expect budgets to soar as soon as you start thinking about modern twin-cam engines such as this Zetec lump. Older Fiat is an option though. Below: If a car needs painting then allow for it in your budget.

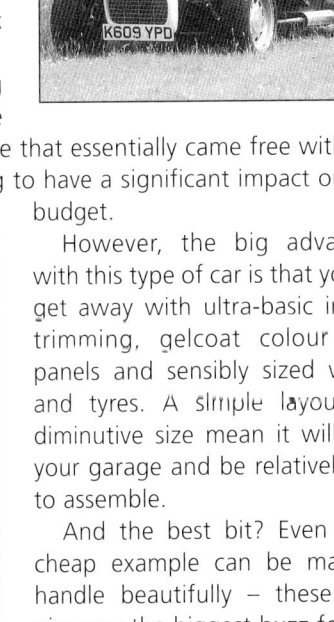

Below: Formula 27 used to be a budget Lotus Seven inspired kit car, but not anymore. It was the first company to develop a bike-engined car of this type.

13

Replicas

Typical build costs: £7,000-20,000
Prime contenders within our budget: Paul Banham Sprint and Spyder.
Cost Escalators: Typical replica finishing items.

Building a replica of a car you otherwise couldn't afford has

Top: Mini-based Banham Sprint is one of the very few kit car replicas that will fall within our budget. Below: Cars such as this beautiful Jaguar-based XK120 replica are well into five figures.

always been a big appeal of the kit car scene. Obviously, the Cobra replica market takes the biggest slice of the action in this sector, hence the reason why we've dealt with it separately, but there are still loads of other lookalikes to consider, from sensational Lancia Stratos kits to the predictable Ferrari fakes and sumptuous Jaguar replicas.

The biggest problem for us tends to be the expense involved in making these cars look convincing. Ferrari replicas need expensive interiors, big wheels and a mid-engined layout that inevitably increases costs (plumbing and cooling problems, special gear linkages, more complex suspension problems to overcome). Replicas of older cars, such as a Jaguar SS100 or D-Type tend to use expensive Jaguar donor components and, in the case of the SS100, lots of brightwork detailing and lovely interior trim.

By and large you are going to struggle in this sector, with only the Paul Banham body conversions offering any real option. This company's replicas of the Porsche 550 Spyder and Austin Healey Sprite being based on a butchered Skoda and Metro respectively.

Traditional tourers

Typical build costs: £6000-£15,000
Prime contenders within our budget: Tempest.
Cost Escalators: Typical chrome brightwork, fancy interiors, paint.

Left: Traditional tourers are often expensive because of the chrome and stainless finishing touches that make them look so special. Above: Marlin Sportster could be one of the few within our budget.

You'd think that a traditional tourer could well be an affordable kit car to consider. After all, they often use comparatively humble donor cars, but the reality with most kits in the sector is that they fall way beyond our budget. Not only can the bodywork be expensive to produce because it is made up of several different panels rather than a single mould, but aluminium louvred bonnets tend to enforce a full paint job rather than use of a factory-supplied gelcoat colour finish.

If that wasn't bad enough, the biggest killer of all tends to be the finishing touches. Traditional tourers need loads of chrome and stainless steel if they are to look convincing and these items are rarely cheap. A convincing interior is also a critical element to finishing off a period roadster. A walnut dashboard is de rigueur, while it will inevitably have to be peppered with glinting aftermarket gauges and switches (none of which can usually be found on a modern donor car).

The bottom line is that we suspect very few models fall into our budget. The Reliant-based Tempest is one of the few.

Below: Motorbike engines first started to appear in the kit car scene via three-wheelers such as this BRA.

Three-wheelers

Typical build costs: £3000-£8000
Prime contenders within our budget: Lomax 223, Blackjack Avion, BRA.
Cost Escalators: Non-donor engines, period detailing.

The three-wheeler market is remarkably popular within the kit car scene, with a wide and varied selection of largely small-scale manufacturers. The big exception to this rule is Lomax, which has produced its Citroen 2CV kits for many years and in simply vast quantities.

When we talk about three-wheelers in the kit car market we generally mean cars with one wheel at the back rather than at the front like a Robin Reliant. As such, these cars

Below: Lomax 223 is the car that made three-wheelers such a trend. 1000s have been sold over the years and the Citroen-based car falls well within our budget.

Above: Not all three-wheelers are cheap. This BMW-based Grinnall looks fab and will cost you over £10,000.

Above: Fisher Fury is one of the more affordable sports cars, especially in Spyder form. You can find out more in Chapter 9.

can be extremely stable and performance, particularly if you end up using a motorbike engine, can be breathtaking. Prime donor car for many of the more affordable options is the previously mentioned Citroen 2CV and this super-cheap donor car can supply just about everything needed to build the kit including, in some cases, the chassis.

Another major appeal for us is the fact that most three-wheelers (so long as they don't end up weighing more than 410kgs) are currently exempt from the Single Vehicle Approval test (saving a healthy £150). What's more, because the cars don't have to go through the test the builder doesn't have to be quite so meticulous about fitting sometimes expensive SVA-friendly items – so there may well be extra savings here. Most three-wheelers will also

Below: Autotune Gemini is one of the industry's long-term success stories. Can be built on a tight budget using either Escort or Sierra components.

qualify for a reduced road tax because of their smaller engines, which means yet more savings when it comes to running the end product.

This quirky marketplace can throw up some really fun and alternative machinery, and three-wheelers tend to have a charm all to themselves. In terms of cost escalators there's not too much to worry about here, except if you opt for an alternative engine to that which came with your donor or if your car has a particular period feel to it and requires those expensive finishing touches we highlighted in earlier sections. Check out Chapter 16 for the full rundown of potential candidates.

Sports cars

Typical build costs: £6,000-£12,000
Prime contenders within our budget: Fisher Fury Spyder, Autotune Gemini, Midas Gold convertible.

Cost Escalators: Non-donor engines, suspension upgrades, paint and trim, wheels and tyres.

This sector of the market is rather open to interpretation and there are a large number of manufacturers

Below: Midas Gold Convertible is a terrific looking Metro-based kit worthy of consideration.

that probably qualify. The biggest problem for us is finding one that can be built within our budget and, as such, our options become somewhat limited. Sports car kits tend to have a fairly substantial amount of bodywork which often includes doors – that immediately makes the cost of production greater than, for example, a Lotus Seven inspired replica.

By its very nature, a sports car needs to be reasonably quick and handle well, and that means a well-honed chassis with a suitably capable suspension system – yet again it's not the cheapest thing to develop. However, there are one or two options open to us. Generally speaking, these will have a fairly basic level of interior trim and bodywork may be more simple. Fisher's stripped-out Fury Spyder is a typical option.

Problems start to arise in this sector as soon as you get carried away and head for a different engine source, decide on a full interior trim package or opt for monster 17" wheels and tyres.

Body conversions

Typical build costs: £3000-£8000
Prime contenders within our budget: Banham X21 and Superbug, JAS Buggy and other buggy kits, GP Spyder, Dakar
Cost Escalators: Donor car repairs

Above: The archetypal body conversion. JAS Buggy is great fun and reviewed in detail in Chapter 11

Body conversions to existing cars used to be a primary part of the kit car world, with VW Beetle floorpans and Triumph Herald and Spitfire chassis forming the basis for a myriad of different models. Kits such as the VW-based beach buggies and the supercar-inspired Nova were prime movers in bringing the kit car scene to a wider audience in the

Below: You wouldn't expect a Range Rover-based body conversion to come within our budget, but the wacky and highly capable Dakar will.

We can't hope to cover every kit car that you can consider on a budget. One way of seeing lots of kits in one place is to visit a kit car show.

Seventies. But it all rather died a death by the mid-Eighties and seemed long forgotten before the onset of Single Vehicle Approval in 1998.

Body conversions have always been exempt from SVA on the basis that the kits don't so much use a donor car but are, as the name suggests, merely conversions to the original production car's bodywork. As such, you can't really retest something that has already passed existing Type Approval regulations. While that premise still holds true for Beetle-based cars using unmodified floorpans, the authorities are closing in on those kits which require a more modern donor car's monocoque structure to be cut and modified. While it currently appears open to interpretation, at worst it means that these cars may have to go through the test after all.

However, the onset of SVA has unquestionably re-lit the body conversion candle and there are now quite a variety of cars available within this sector and crossing over into other sectors we've already dealt with (such as Pontiac Fiero and Toyota MR2-based Ferrari replicas).

Generally speaking, most body conversions (with the exception of those we've just mentioned) can be completed within our budget but you shouldn't underestimate the work and expense that may be incurred getting the donor components into a serviceable condition. Old VW Beetle floorpans will always require welding work while many of the other components may need significant refurbishment or complete rebuilding.

So these are not necessarily easy projects and if you're not confident with welding techniques or fibreglassing and body preparation, this could be a more costly exercise than you thought.

Finding out more

Obviously we can't go through every kit car currently on the market and that's not our intention. To get a better idea of what types of cars are available and which companies are actively promoting their products you should get hold of a few copies of *Which Kit?* magazine and also a copy of its annual guides, the *Which Kit? Guide* and the *Complete Guide To Kit Cars*.

Beyond that, it's vital that you visit one or two of the big annual kit car shows, such as Stoneleigh in May and Donington in September. There's nothing like seeing these cars in the flesh, although leave your chequebook firmly at home if you want to avoid getting thoroughly carried away! Finally, we've tried to outline what we feel are all the main movers and shakers in the sub five-grand bracket in Chapter 16.

Chapter Three

Choosing the right car

(within your budget and ability)

It's all very well being adamant that only a Cobra replica will do and, if you weld your own chassis and fabricate your own aluminium body, you'll be on the road for under your budget of £5000, but are you really being realistic? Being sensible about the kind of car you want to build (and its specification) and making an honest assessment of your own skills will be vital if you want to come in on budget and, even more importantly, actually complete the project.

How capable are you?

With an ample budget it's fair to say you can build any kit car you like, because if there's an area of the build you can't manage yourself, you can always pay someone else to do it. More expensive kits have also been more comprehensively developed, so they are usually a bit more straightforward to build in the first place. Better quality moulds mean fibreglass panels are

Above: It's not just price that makes the Lotus Seven inspired kit car so popular – it's also the ideal project for the first time builder.

more accurate while bespoke components have been specifically designed for the job rather than modified from an old Cortina.

So, turn that on its head and, while it's not true to say that all cheap kits are difficult to build, it may often be the case that the enthusiast is left with more work to do himself. At its most simple, that may mean painting the chassis for rust protection rather than opting for the factory powder-coated finish. At its most complicated, it may mean welding the chassis together yourself from a pile of tubes!

Before you even begin looking around at your kit options, you need to ask yourself a few questions about what you are prepared to do yourself and what you want done for you by someone else. These might include...

● *Do you want to weld up your*

Below: Be realistic about your budget and your ability. A Cobra replica may be your dream car, but building one on a tight budget will be very tricky.

Above: The Locost can be built from a book, but are you up to welding your own chassis? Buying a pre-fabricated, but more expensive chassis may be more realistic.

own chassis or buy a ready built chassis and bodywork package?

● *Are you happy to source the donor components and*

Below: Working to a tight budget, you may have to strip down and refurbish components from an old donor car. Some companies, such as Tiger Racing, offer pre-stripped donor packs.

then refurbish them or would you rather opt for a professionally reconditioned suspension package from a specialist?

● *Will you need to rebuild an engine yourself?*

● *If you want trim in the car, are you prepared to make it or would you rather buy it pre-done.?*

● *Are you happy using a modified version of the donor's wiring loom or do you want the bespoke aftermarket item offered by the manufacturer etc, etc?*

The chances are that if you want to come in under our budget of five grand you will have to do more of the basic spadework than you would if you had a greater amount of cash in the bank. Above all else, you need to be realistic about what you feel capable of achieving.

What sort of car do you want?

Having come to some sort of decision as to what you can realistically expect to achieve yourself, choosing the right kit car in the first place will also ease your quest.

Try to build an essentially expensive kit car on a tight

Left: Big wheels, fancy engines and leather interiors cost big bucks. Above: No such problems with this back to basics buggy.

budget and you'll have to be more creative about where you source parts and undertake more work yourself. Opt for a simple kit car that was always designed to be assembled for next to nothing and you'll have fewer surprises and be less pushed when it comes to paying for all the necessary components. You may also find that you can then afford those nice finishing touches that you'd have to forego on the more expensive kit.

On a tight budget you really need to be realistic about the spec of the car and what you'll be able to achieve. All those fancy trim items you saw on the professionally painted company demo car (sat on its 17" wheels, with full leather interior and 5.7-litre Chevrolet V8 engine) will soon eat into your budget. If you're not prepared to build an example without these components, then you're best looking elsewhere.

Building a cheap car needn't be difficult unless you choose to make it that way by selecting an unsuitable project or setting yourself unrealistic levels of fit and finish. But how do you know whether a project will be easy or difficult and whether or not it can realistically be built within your budget?

Do your homework

The first thing you need to do is get a good understanding of what cars are available within any one style of kit car that you fancy.

So if it's Lotus Seven inspired replicas that turn you on, you need to get hold of a few copies of *Which Kit?* magazine and ask for brochures from all the likely contenders.

Brochures – Brochures can tell you a great deal about the product and the company behind it. At this budget end of the market you shouldn't be too worried whether the paperwork is a scruffy photocopy or fancy printed job – what we're looking for here are details. How is the kit supplied? Is it offered in individual items or sold as a comprehensive package...

If it's the latter, just how comprehensive is it? Don't assume that it'll include weather gear or even a windscreen until you've checked! If it genuinely seems quite comprehensive then you can use it as a checklist

Below: Not all kit packages are the same – check the brochure details carefully and look at the pictures to see what additional goodies have been added to the cars.

21

Left: Big shows offer a great opportunity to see several different cars all in one place. Above: They're also ideal for checking out specific cars in detail and meeting staff members.

when comparing prices from those companies that only supply the kit in bits. A quick total-up of the individual items may well give you a shock and the comprehensive kit may actually be cheaper even though it initially appears quite expensive.

You can also check the component list in the brochure against any pictures of completed cars that come with it. More often than not you'll find that the pictures quickly identify extra things not included within the price list and which may not be on your standard donor car – different engines, exhausts, trim specs, instruments, switches, lights, wheels and tyres, wing mirrors, seat belts etc, etc. It's not the end of the world, so long as you realise that your budget may not allow for these 'luxuries' unless you source them in some other way.

While these brochures will soon tell you whether or not you are on the right track in terms of build costs, they'll also highlight different styles of interior, engine options, suspension systems and body styles – it's a good way of whittling down what type of car you really want.

Shows – Next stop is to get along to one or two kit car shows. This is a great way to see several different makes all in one place but do check before you go that the manufacturers you really want to see will be attending. It's also a chance to get a first impression of some of the company's staff and poke about the demo cars to see whether or not you like what you see.

Looking over these cars up close is an ideal opportunity to quickly evaluate whether a car has been built on a budget or up to a show spec. More often than not, company demo cars tend to head for the latter route, but as you get more experienced you'll quickly be able to identify the features that you can do without and those that you feel you really must have.

By now you'll be getting a pretty good idea of which

Club stands are great for seeing how private enthusiasts have built their cars. The owners are always happy to show you around and tell you of any problems.

22

cars are potential projects and which will have to be consigned to the dustbin because of excessive build costs or simply because you don't like the styling, or whatever.

Owners' clubs – Getting in contact with the relevant owners' club can be a great way of getting the real story on how easy or difficult a project will be. Existing owners aren't trying to sell you anything and, if something went wrong, they'll be the first to tell you. But not only will the relevant owners' club dish the dirt on any common problems, it's also a great source of build advice and contacts for where to find those elusive parts cheaply.

Of course, many owners are very happy to tell you how much or little they spent and, if the average build cost is way over your budget, you have to ask yourself whether it's going to be possible to build it much more cheaply.

Some owners' clubs are much more active than others and that also gives you a good indication of the number of kits that have been sold. We've listed all the contacts for relevant clubs at the back of this book in Appendix D.

Factory visit – Fired up with enthusiasm and full of information, now's the time for that factory visit. But what can you expect to see when you appear at a company's workshop? Unless you've suddenly landed a big inheritance and are looking to the top of the industry, don't expect anything too flashy. While the likes of Westfield and Caterham's premises are genuinely impressive, by far the majority of operations within the kit car scene operate out of small and sometimes scruffy industrial units.

Below: Is the factory busy? Lots of activity shows a thriving company.

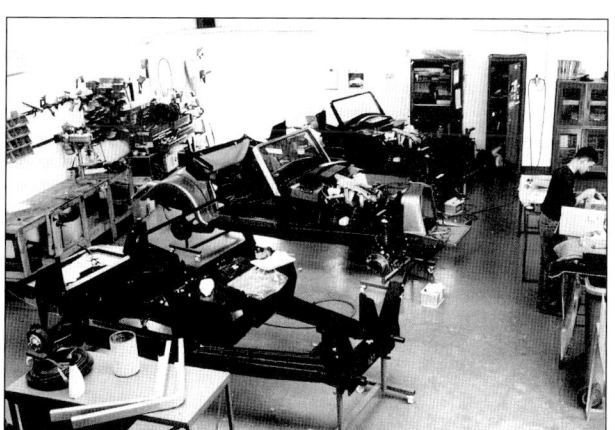

Above: A factory visit is for when things get more serious – time to meet the owner and go for a test drive. Below: Don't expect all factories to be as big and impressive as Westfield.

The number of staff around will typically vary from just one or two up to perhaps ten. Some companies build their chassis and bodies on site, but others may use outside contractors for the fabrication work, simply bringing together the completed components at the factory.

Don't always expect to be able to drive the factory demo car but do get yourself taken out for a test drive by one of the staff and then, most importantly, have a good sit in the driving seat once you're back at base. This will soon tell you whether the driving position is any good, whether the pedals are well spaced, how wide the footwell is, whether the handbrake is in the way, whether the steering is a little high or sat between your knees. Some of these things you may be able to adjust in your own build but, by and large, we'd expect a driving position to suit most drivers so long as the seat is adjustable.

Above: Be careful how you spend your limited funds. Don't blow it all on the suspension and engine and then find you've got nothing left for the bodywork etc.

As we've already mentioned, the demo car will usually show how far the product can be taken, rather than demonstrate how cheaply it can be built. So you need to get your sensible head on for a minute and have a proper look around the car to see how much this car would probably cost to build. What things are you happy to do without or perhaps source second-hand rather than new?

Now that you're here, make sure you see how the chassis and bodies are presented to the builder. Is there a large parts department or is everything bought in from elsewhere as and when it's needed – if it is you may have to wait some time for certain parts when you come to order them.

Is the factory busy? A single dusty bodyshell and an empty chassis jig (the frame in which the chassis is welded together) indicate a quiet company struggling for sales. More affordable kits, by their very nature, require a reasonable volume of sales for the manufacturer to make ends meet, so in an ideal world you're looking for lots of completed chassis and bodies stacked up awaiting collection later in the week.

The final thing you should be looking out for is how well you get on with the main man and his staff. With the more affordable end of the market where volumes can be high, it's unrealistic to expect everyone to be massively interested in your big plans – they're seeing a lot of potential customers, not all of whom will go on to buy a kit. However, you should feel confident in the people you are dealing with.

How are the phones being answered while you're there? Are those existing customers being dealt with or is the answerphone on? You will need to speak to the factory during your build, either to ask questions or simply to order parts, and you must be confident that someone is going to deal with you promptly and courteously.

Your budget

In the next chapter we'll have a look at some of the ancillary costs you may have to consider beyond the purchase of the parts that go to make up a car, but for the moment we are just going to consider the specific build costs.

We're constantly mentioning this magic figure of £5000 and it's a figure which we feel will allow you a reasonable choice of cars to choose from and a sum which should allow you to build a car you can be proud of. Of course, what is doesn't mean is that you need £5000 in the bank before you start. This project is going to take you some time to complete – probably a minimum of six months and perhaps well over a year. You won't necessarily be buying everything at once (unless you opt for a comprehensive kit package) so you can spread out your budget over the period of the build to ease the strain on your bank balance.

The first thing you probably need to do is get hold of a suitable donor car and then strip it down and refurbish the parts accordingly. None of this need cost you more than a few hundred pounds, so it eases you into the project gently, but you will have larger expenses later on. It's therefore vital that you don't get too carried away at this stage and spend your cash uprating the brakes and suddenly deciding that you need a 200bhp rebuilt engine.

Below: Don't forget you can always upgrade later on. These wheels came free with the donor but can be replaced with alloys when funds allow.

We come across a large number of kit cars that look a complete mess because the owner has put all his money into the suspension and then run out of money for the vital finishing touches. So watch out, spreading your budget makes complete sense, but make sure you do it wisely.

If you're really struggling for cash, then it's always tempting to say that you'll take longer over the build to give yourself more chance of saving up the necessary funds. If this is the only way you can afford the kit, then go with it, but building a car takes a lot of dedication and it's easy to get bogged down and lose enthusiasm if the project is moving at a snail's pace. We've little doubt that a vast number of kit cars never reach completion simply because the builder has lost interest. If you can, keep everything ticking along nicely and set yourself targets by which you must complete certain sections of the build.

We've talked a lot so far in this book about having to make sacrifices when it comes to the specification of your car – simple trim, cheaper alloys, basic engine spec, etc etc. But it's very important to remember that you can always upgrade these items at a later stage, after the car has hit the road. While a set of painted steel wheels will get you on the road, you can always move on to the fancy alloys next year. If you've opted for a completely bare interior to start with, then a good winter project in twelve months' time might be to pull out the existing seats and trim out the inside in the carpet you really wanted. Steering wheels can be upgraded, as can seats

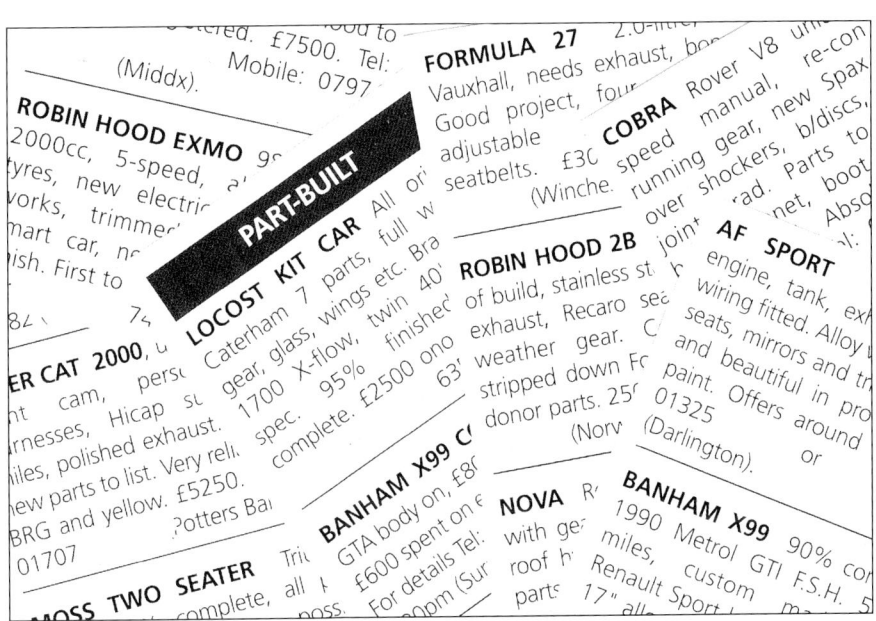

Above: Don't let your project take so long that it never reaches completion and becomes a part-built bargain in the classifieds.

and almost everything else in the interior, and much the same goes for the engine bay...

The 2-litre Pinto engine that came free with your Sierra donor will do fine for now but as more funds become available you might then want to add a couple of fat Weber carbs or have the cylinder head uprated with a new camshaft. All are extremely easy upgrades that can be done at any time in the future. So while we constantly go on about being realistic in terms of your initial build specification, there's nothing to say that in two year's time you might have achieved the dream car that previously was out of reach.

25

Chapter Four

Ancillary Expenditure

OK, so we've set ourselves a budget of £5000. But does that mean you've got £5000 to spend on parts for the car or is that your complete budget for the project? There are other costs to consider beyond the basic components that go to make up a kit and, while it may be that you don't consider these as part of your build budget, it's still cash coming out of your bank account.

Setting up costs

Before you even get a chassis in your garage (or the tubes that go to make up a chassis if you're really starting at the beginning!) you need to ensure that you can build this creation safely and, since you'll be spending some time doing it, in some degree of comfort. Below are just one or two of the basic items we feel are vital to a successful and pleasant kit car building experience.

Electricity: You'll definitely need some of this, either supplied from a mains electricity supply or, if you're working in a lock-up, from a generator. At its most basic,

Below: A substantial workbench and a big vice are vital garage equipment.

Above: Getting some decent lighting and electrical supply is important if the build is to be enjoyable.

you could be looking at additional wiring and plugs.

Tools: It goes without saying that you'll need a few tools and many of us will already have assembled together basic socket sets, screwdrivers and the like. Essential things you may not have might include a workbench, a substantial bench-mounted vice, files, tin snips and other electrical goodies such as a drill, angle grinder or jigsaw.

Light: Lock-ups don't usually come with any lighting and you'll find it a real struggle if you have to rely on pushing the car outside in order to work on it. Even a proper garage beside the house may only have a single strip light and getting some decent lighting will really make the build process easier and safer.

Insurance: Over the period of a typical kit car build you will have assembled components that will eventually equate to your total build budget, so it makes sense that these components should be insured, doesn't it? Thankfully, build-up insurance needn't cost the earth, but not all insurers offer such

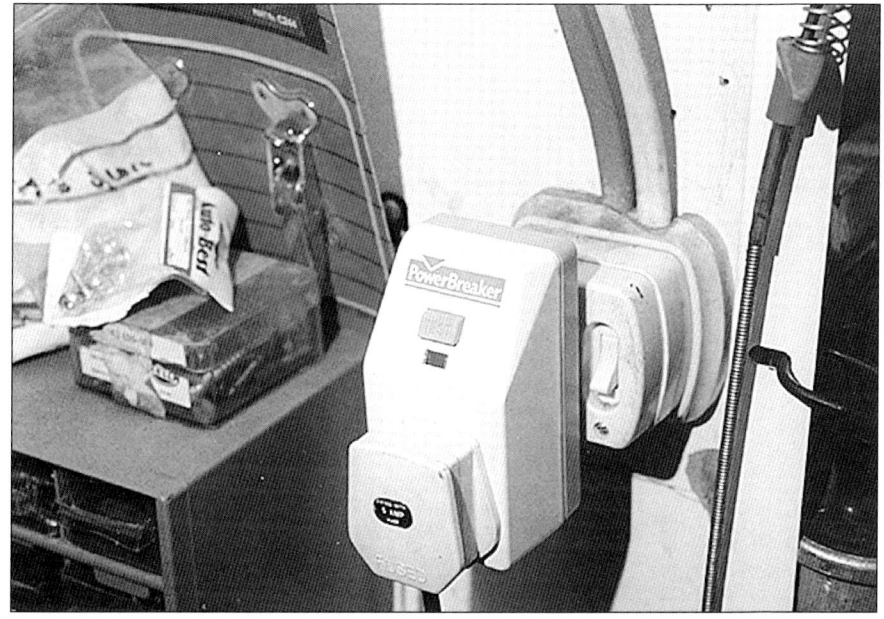

Left: Be extremely careful working underneath the chassis and use decent axle stands or trestles. Note the jack remains in place for additional security. Above: Circuit breaker is another vital purchase.

cover and you need to be careful about exactly how comprehensive any cover will be. Quotes are usually based on the value of the finished car and are payable annually. As a guide, around £50-£80/annum should cover our £5000 investment.

Safety first

Before anything else, you must ensure your own safety, and there are some simple ways of avoiding any nasty accidents.

Electrical hazards: If you're not confident with putting in extra wiring or lighting, then you must get a professional in to do the job properly. Mains electricity won't just give you a jolt – it can kill. The same applies when you're using any electrical tools in the garage. You must use a circuit breaker in the socket at all times. If you then accidentally cut through the power cable to your angle grinder the circuit breaker will cut the power before you get seriously harmed. While these can be cheap, we've always been advised that the more expensive ones are better.

Hand, eye and mouth protection: Using a grinder, jigsaw or any kind of cutting or sanding implement carries inherent dangers. A heavy pair of gloves, proper eye protection and a decent face mask (with changeable filters) are all things you need to buy before starting a project.

Fire hazards: Not only will you be using flammable paints (that should be kept outside when not in use), but you may well have a full tank of fuel and oily rags scattered about the floor. All of which are at risk of igniting if you end up using an angle grinder or welder or when you come to start the car for the first time or check the electrics. A large capacity fire extinguisher capable of dealing with both electrical and fuel fires is a pretty wise investment. If the garage is attached to your house a smoke alarm is another primary purchase.

Working under the chassis: A set of four axle stands or two substantial trestles will be another crucial purchase.

Below: A decent face mask, with changeable filters, is important. Better eye protection than shown here is also vital.

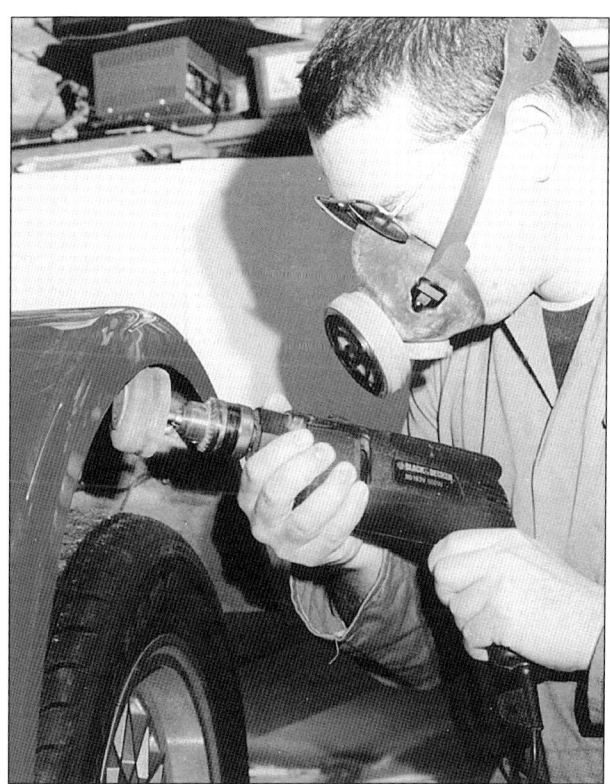

Building the car isn't your only expense. An SVA test will set you back an additional £150 and £30 extra for a retest should you fail.

Piling up a few bricks on which to stand a bare chassis simply will not do. It's also worth placing a spare wheel under the chassis whenever you're working on it as a further safety net should the worst happen and your newly welded trestles suddenly give way.

The costs involved in setting up your garage and making sure you're safe can quickly mount up and, whether or not you consider these to be part of your build budget, they are just as important (and more so) than those fancy wheels and tyres you wanted.

Costs after the car is complete

As with those setting up and safety costs we've dealt with above, you may consider the outlay incurred after your car is complete to be separate from your build budget. However, your bank manager may think otherwise!

Single Vehicle Approval: This is a test that just about every kit car must go through before you can register it and drive it legally on the road. While there are one or two exceptions, we'll assume your kit will be required to go through the test. As such you'll immediately be looking at £150 for the test itself and, if you fail on your first attempt, £30 for a retest.

First registration fee: No getting away from this one, but at least the damage is limited to just £25.

Road Tax: On a first registration you have to tax the car for a full year rather than getting away with just six months, so that's a further £160.

Insurance: Thankfully kit car insurance is usually one of those welcome surprises when compared to your everyday runaround. Limited mileage policies are the norm and premiums can sometimes be encouragingly low. However, make sure you use one of the kit car specialists since the likes of Direct Line and AA Insurance won't know what you're talking about!

Fuel: It sounds pretty obvious, doesn't it, but don't under-estimate the amount of fuel that a thirsty V8 will get through when you're using it hard. Modern injection engines will be far more economical but it's certainly something you should consider when deciding which car you want to build.

Budgeting for the build itself is a black art at the best of times and dependent not only on the cost of components but also the degree to which you are prepared to do the work yourself. In the next chapter we point out a few money-saving tips...

Chapter Five

Tricks of the trade

Building a kit car on a strict budget means you need to be imaginative when it comes to building the car and sourcing those parts that don't actually come with the kit or donor car.

Kit tricks

While it's fair to say that 98% of the industry works on the basis of supplying a customer with a pre-fabricated chassis and body, there are a few companies who will happily supply you with paper plans so that you can build your own. Make no mistake, this isn't for the fainthearted, but it is certainly one way to get a kit car on the road for the absolute minimum of outlay.

Currently grabbing much of the attention is the Ron Champion book, *Build Your Own Sports Car For As Little As £250*, which explains in some detail how to fabricate a chassis and make fibreglass body panels and produce a car firmly in the Lotus Seven inspired replica mould. If the challenge of welding up your own chassis forms part of the appeal of the build then all well and good, but a number of companies now offer these same chassis pre-fabricated and at amazingly competitive prices.

For all your effort, you may not be saving that much cash and will have a chassis of questionable integrity unless you're really confident of your own welding skills. Much the same can be said for the fibreglass panels, with a number of companies now offering suitable panels at what must almost be the cost of manufacture.

But the Locost phenomenon is far from the first to offer a self-build option for the chassis and body. A number of other manufacturers have been supplying plans for home assembly for many years, namely BWE with its Locust. In the case of this example, a basic ladderframe chassis is supplied by the factory but the complete bodywork is made either from marine ply or MDF and it can then be covered with a very thin sheet of aluminium for an authentic metal finish. The end result can look great and is usually impressively rigid, if a little heavy.

Of course, making your own chassis and body is taking things to extremes, but you can still make a few savings with the basic kit purchase by perhaps avoiding the bulk packages or simply asking for the chassis in bare

Above and below: Locost kit car is based around a book from which enthusiasts can build everything, including their own chassis. Read more about it in Chapter 12.

Above: Depending on the donor, it can be easy to upgrade the brakes. This caliper could be rebuilt.

Above: This side indicator would work well on a kit.

metal rather than with a costly powder-coated finish. Painting at home can provide a decent rust protective coating if done quickly and comprehensively.

Donor tricks

Becoming something of a Junkyard Junky will be vital if

To build a car on a budget you'll need to be a Junkyard Junkie.

you're going to come in on budget. While your donor car may supply many of the components you'll need for the build, there will often be other parts that must be found from elsewhere. Some of these will be vital components in order to make the car work, such as a different shaped radiator, but others may be finishing items that are more aesthetically pleasing than the things found on your donor car, such as side indicators, gear lever gaiters, gear knobs etc.

Finding a decent car breaker will really be vital to getting all these parts affordably and some will specialise

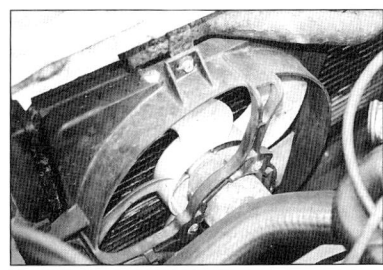

Above: Electric fans from alternative donors are a cheap upgrade. Right: Older donors can offer good instruments, but don't discount clocks, etc from more modern cars.

in newer cars while others will have older offerings. Before you make a visit, write a list of all the things you need to look for and any vital measurements that need to be adhered to. Bring along a decent set of tools and don't forget a few pairs of inspection gloves – these will really help to keep your hands clean because not all scrap yards have great washing facilities (if at all!). You don't want to be getting back into your own car covered in oil and mud.

So what things can you expect to find in a scrap yard that will enhance your kit car and avoid the need to buy new parts?

Mechanical parts – While your donor should hopefully have supplied a basic set of suspension components, a visit to the scrap yard may offer some cheap upgrades.

Aftermarket rear view mirrors are usually horrid. Production ones are much better.

Below: Some of these switches might be useful.

Vented discs and calipers instead of solid discs, different rear differential ratios, uprated carburettors for your engine, bigger brake servos etc, etc. All can enhance your car's basic specification at minimal expense.

Radiators – The restricted space in many kit car engine bays often means that the standard donor radiator won't fit. While the kit manufacturer will probably recommend one that does, a quick visit to the scrap yard might reveal a second-hand one in serviceable condition. Alternatively, you might even find a higher capacity radiator that offers improved cooling from the one recommended.

Above: Aftermarket seats can be very expensive. Retrimming these Renault 5 items would be comparatively cheap.

Cooling fans – There's always a temptation here to buy an aftermarket electric fan simply because your old Ford Cortina has an engine-driven unit. But just about every production car on the planet now comes with an electronically operated electric fan, so get along to the scrappy and have a dig around to find the neatest one you can. They'll nearly always be in serviceable condition.

Instruments – Not many modern cars have attractive instrumentation and very few will offer the individual period style gauges most kit cars are designed for. Dig around your nearest scrappy and the chances are that you'll come across an old Triumph somewhere which might throw up some or all of the gauges that you want. Old Jaguars are another possibility while you shouldn't ignore surprises such as older Fiats and, believe it or not, Ladas!

Switches – The older cars we've mentioned above are also just perfect for supplying really good rocker switches to operate windscreen wipers, headlights, heater and other ancillaries. In fact these are invariably much better made than brand new aftermarket items and will always cause interest when people look over your car at shows.

Seat runners – While most production car seats are too wide for use in kit cars (although Triumph Spitfire units can be perfect), you may well find a natty pair of seat runners. Those Ladas we mentioned earlier are just perfect, but many other older cars may throw up useful alternatives.

Interior lights – An interior light isn't exactly vital, but it can be a nice finishing touch while, if you're not so confident about your work (!), you can always put one in the engine bay to help see when things go wrong at night!

Mirrors – Decent wing mirrors and central rear view mirrors are all now compulsory items for the Single Vehicle Approval test, but don't feel you must buy an aftermarket one. Metro wing mirrors are used on many modern kit cars, while the old Mini will throw up some more period looking versions. Unless you're after a chromed interior mirror, you'll also find production car rear view mirrors considerably more substantial than aftermarket ones.

Gear knobs – An expensive Momo gear knob might be nice but you'll be surprised what you can find in the production car world. Look into the more executive cars and you'll come up with some excellent ones, although you may need to be a bit ingenious about how you fit it to your gear lever. A leather gear lever surround always looks the part but many rubber gear lever surrounds also look good and can be made to fit a flat centre tunnel easily.

Side indicators – Side indicators form part of your MoT test and there are now some really great production car side repeaters to choose from. The oval Ford ones come in a variety of different shapes and colour tones, but other nice ones to consider might include Honda, Citroen/Peugeot and VW. The latest Ford Focus triangular ones are also pretty groovy!

Fuse boxes and electrical items – If the fuse box that came with your donor car is too large or has corroded badly, then the scrap yard is certainly where you'll need to head. Not only will you be able to get yourself a load of spare fuses but older cars will often have comparatively simple fuse boxes which are ideal for use in a kit car.

Rubber grommets and other parts – Look around any modern car and there are rubber bump stops and grommets everywhere. Where looms pass through a bulkhead there will inevitably be a rubber grommet to stop the wiring being frayed against the metal and these can be perfect for use in a kit car loom where it's passing through the front aluminium bulkhead. Rubber bonnet stops can also be useful for maintaining the panel gap on kit car boot lids.

Knowing where to look

Half the battle with any kit car is knowing where to look for those seemingly elusive parts or services. Before you resort to a real bodge-up, have a look around a few cars at kit car shows and see how other people have done the job. Once you know what looks good, then you've got to find the fixings, glue, parts or whatever to do it just as well.

Kit car shows are a great place to find parts when you wander through the accessory stands, from plastic cable ties to second-hand chrome-bezelled gauges; you'll come across most things at the larger kit car events.

For new items then it's worth assembling a decent selection of brochures from the likes of Europa Spares and Demon Tweaks. Carpet suppliers will often have a stand at the kit car shows, but you can also buy direct

Above: For cleaner parts scavenging, try the accessory traders at any typical kit car show.

from them using their own catalogues. People such as Woolies are just perfect for this sort of stuff as well as specialist rubber items like door and window seals. Check out Appendix C for a comprehensive list of contacts.

Autojumbles are another worthwhile venue and, if you keep your eyes open, you can often come across second-hand Lotus and Caterham wings and nose cones that can be used on your own replica.

Something that few builders really take advantage of is their local engineering shops, which can have large supplies of aluminium sheeting and chassis tubing and who can also undertake more specialist bending and welding jobs. Invariably these guys seem extremely competitively priced...

And then there are those fancy powder-coated, anodised and chrome finishes that some builders make the most of on their cars. Despite the fact that they often look a million dollars, these can be extremely cheap if you take in a decent number of parts to get done all at one time. The same places will usually have a sand-blasting facility, which is just perfect for getting a really professional clean up on all your grubby donor suspension parts.

Dig out all these places before you start your build (*Yellow Pages* is a good source of contacts) and you'll then be really prepared when the opportunities arise to give your car a fancy finishing touch for not very much money.

Chapter Six

Tiger Cat

The company

Walk into Tiger Racing's Cambridgeshire base and the workshop isn't just brimming with Tigers in various different states of completion, it also plays host to a veritable bevy of Dudleys. While several kit car companies could claim to be family run operations, Tiger Racing takes the concept to a whole new level...

Top dog (although wife Sue might well disagree!) is Jim Dudley, MD and founder of Tiger Racing, who's ably assisted by the aforementioned Sue who controls the company's large parts department and the assembly of kit packages. Their son Paul keeps an eye on the bodywork side of the business, prototyping of new models and overseeing fully built cars. Then there's daughter, Laura, who makes up the interior trim packages (along with Jim's mum, Milly) and manages the paperwork. Finally there's Paul's wife, Sarah, who deals with accounts.

If the truth be known, it seems they're all rushing around like mad things most of the time, doing whatever needs to be done to keep a busy company (and its customers) on track. Actually, if there's one thing that does come across from our regular visits to Tiger's Wisbech base, it's that everyone works extremely hard and is hugely enthusiastic about the end product. Not that things have always gone smoothly for one of the

Above: Jim Dudley fronts a family run business that is now one of the industry's largest.

Below: The car that nearly ended it all. South African RM7 import put Tiger on the end of a legal writ from both Caterham and Westfield.

UK's larger manufacturers...

Jim Dudley's first foray into the kit car business in 1989 could so easily have been his last. Already running a successful garage business specialising in VWs, Jim's long-time enthusiasm for Lotus Sevens (having owned well over 50 of them by then) initially landed him in hot water. "I had a South African guy come to work for me in one of my paint shops," he remembers, "and I was talking to him one lunchtime. He had this South African magazine in his hand and I picked up on a feature with the RM7 in it."

The RM7 was South Africa's attempt at a Caterham replica, and Jim liked the quality of the product. "We imported six cars and then got sued by Caterham and Westfield!" The RM7 was deemed to be on the wrong side of the law and Jim's first venture into the kit car world was over before it had begun - costing him a small fortune in the process.

Dusting himself off from this unexpected legal spat, Jim realised he didn't need to borrow anyone else's design – he had all the equipment and experience to make his own car from scratch. The Tiger Super Six was the result, launched just months later at the Sandown kit car show in 1990.

Keen to establish his car as being utterly unique, the Super Six had a number of distinctive features. "If you look at the Super Six nose it's like a historic BRM – it's not a Lotus Seven nose." comments Jim. "We did the rear wings with the dip on the back like an early Lotus 6 – hence the Super 6 name. Next we wanted the chassis to be radically different from anything produced."

Opting for significantly larger section chassis tubing instantly set the Tiger apart from its competitors. "Since then we've had two cars involved in head-on collisions and one with a very bad side impact, and the chassis has proved itself very strong."

The Super Six was an instant success with enthusiasts, the VW Golf front uprights, vented disc brakes and pressed lower wishbones all helping to establish the product in its own right. The styling was also something of a hit, the distinctive rear wings and bonnet bulge offering enthusiasts a different interpretation of a familiar theme. "We thought we needed to establish a shape," recalls Jim, "establish it as a good little sports car and have it trade marked. So the first thing we did was spend a load of money trade marking the Super Six."

Keeping the product competitively priced was also an early priority. "If you're new on the market and you're

Above: Here's the very first Tiger Six. Note aluminium bonnet and lack of engine hump - changed for production kits.

going to compete, you need to be competitive on your pricing. It wasn't a big thing because we knew we could be competitive."

If the new product was well clear of the courts, by 1996 its spiralling sales success would prove to be the company's next big challenge. "A million pound order nearly put us out of business – that's an unusual statement really, but it's fact," says Jim thoughtfully. Expanding marketing of the Super Six to the lucrative Japanese market had borne fruit and Tiger Racing now had a vast order for complete cars. With two fully built Super Six's leaving the factory every week, the pressure was on...

A move to larger premises was needed and the small,

Below: Distinctive chassis uses larger chassis rails and has proved extremely strong when needed.

Below: Huge Japanese order meant a move to larger premises and a substantial workforce. It nearly crippled the company in huge overheads.

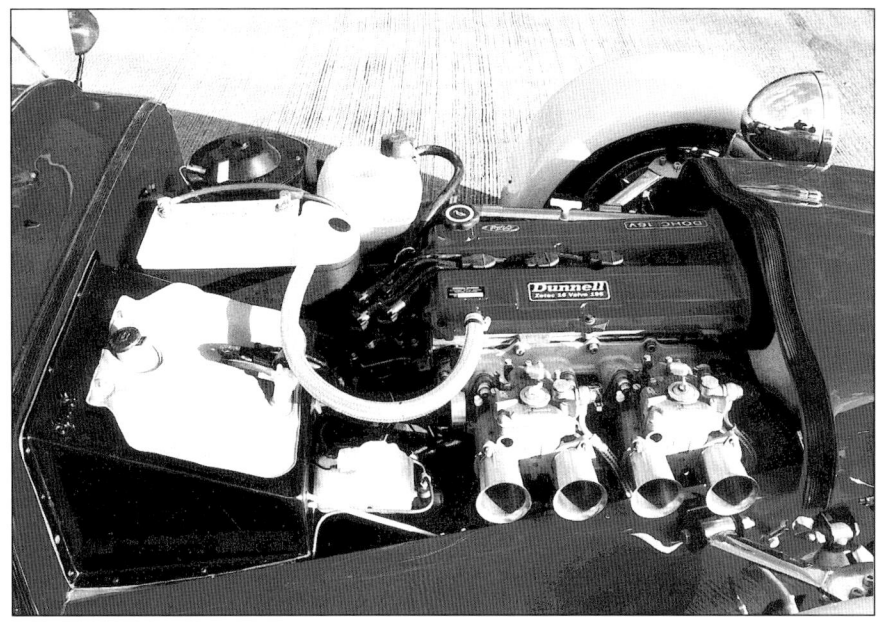

Above: Ford Pinto has always been popular in the Super Six, but cars have seen all manner of different installations, from the modern Ford Zetec (above) to Fiat twin-cam (top right) and Ford X-flow (right).

family run business was soon employing lots of people – the overheads were to prove crippling. "We had sixteen people building cars and a 20,000sq/ft factory which wasn't cheap. And then the Japanese started to change the specification. They'd want us to change something like the tunnel top and it meant we had to stop – people can't build cars when you're redeveloping. Finally, the Japanese sales simply collapsed. It could so easily have been the end."

Dropping everything, Tiger retreated back into its old East London unit, reeling from massive losses but, ironically, with a product now more developed and refined than ever before. It was a bitter blow.

Below: The Tiger Super Six as we know it today. Distinctive rear arches and bonnet bulge continue to make this an aggressive looking performer.

"We looked at what was on the market," says Jim, "and there was no-one at the time offering a kit that could use a complete Sierra." Unwilling to revamp the now well-sorted Super Six, Tiger began with a clean sheet. Reverting back to a more conventional size chassis tube (which was also cheaper to buy), the company developed a product that used as much from the one donor as humanly possible. Initial wariness about denting Super Six sales meant that the new car would once again have some distinctive features, most significantly the Healey Silverstone-inspired front nose cone.

Being all-Sierra based meant the new Tiger Cub was Tiger's first genuinely budget kit car, and it was a factor not missed on those who saw it for the first time at the Donington kit car show in 1995. "We sold twenty or thirty of them straight off," remembers Jim, but almost immediately the new design was coming under fire. "People were asking for a more conventional nose, so eventually we said OK and re-introduced it as the Tiger Cat at Donington 1997.

If the Super Six had established Tiger as a solid mid-range player in the hugely competitive Lotus Seven inspired marketplace, the Cat would transform the company into a major force in the back-to-basics kit car market. Along with offering a conventional body/chassis kit, Tiger soon extended the options to include a comprehensive kit package where the builder only needed a donor Sierra to complete the car. More than that, Tiger was even happy to source the donor components – a pre-stripped donor pack quickly becoming hugely popular with almost 50% of Tiger Cat customers.

With the success of the Cat came further development within the Tiger empire and, while manufacturing premises were initially kept in East London, the operation's main location moved up into the midlands, just outside Peterborough. Here Tiger Racing has continued to cautiously expand to the point where today the company produces over 200 units per year, around 50% of which are devoted to Cat sales.

In amongst volume sellers such as the Super Six and Cat, Tiger Racing has also found time to develop a number of other significant models. Geared more obviously at the upper end of the market, the company once again started with a clean sheet when it set about designing the Tiger R6, an ultimate spec model only available in largely complete kit form. Using a De Dion rear suspension, lightweight chassis and body, and centred around a high performance version of the Ford Zetec engine, it's an awesome performer which was soon joined by Tiger's own interpretation of the bike-powered craze, the ZX9R-engined R6.

Taking this theme to its ultimate conclusion, Tiger joined forced with Z-Cars to manufacture the Z100, a twin bike-engined screamer currently using two ZX12 engines and a 4-wheel-drive transmission to post 0-60mph times of just 2.8 seconds. Having already set an unofficial world-record as the fastest accelerating production car in the world, the Guinness Book Of Records is surely beckoning.

But for the latest chapter in Tiger Racing's seemingly endless onslaught, you have to look back to the late Nineties, when a new threat was emerging – this time in the form of a book. Launched in 1996, Ron Champion's book, *Build Your Own Sports Car For As Little As £250*, was really gathering pace as the Millennium loomed large. People weren't just reading it – they really wanted

Below: Tiger's most serious model is the Z100, complete with not one, but two motorbike engines! Slightly beyond our budget.

Above: Cub was Tiger's first attempt at a low budget car. Healey Silverstone inspired nosecone not to everyone's liking. Tiger Cat (below) soon solved that.

to have a go, and those manufacturers previously offering a conventionally packaged, budget kit car were feeling the pinch.

Jim Dudley was unimpressed by the book, feeling that a Mk2 Escort donor car was old-hat. Not only that, but he also felt he could provide better hands-on advice about the realities of building a car from scratch. Never one to shy away from a challenge, he began wondering whether he might write a book of his own.

At much the same time as these thoughts were going through his mind, Jim was approached by another kit car manufacturer looking to offload its existing product and move out of the industry. While the Lotus Seven inspired Phoenix Avon may have seemed a strange car to buy considering Tiger's existing product range, the new car offered a number of features. Not least of these was the fact that it had a fully independent rear suspension using double wishbones rather than retaining the Sierra's reasonably heavy and cumbersome IRS set-up.

Jim didn't want to use the existing Tiger Cat as the basis for his book since it seemed far wiser to launch it with a new car, not one that was already well established as a conventional kit car. Suddenly the Phoenix Avon began to make more sense than ever. Here was a car which previously had a very low profile within the industry and which also offered an appealing, full IRS rear suspension. Its all-fibreglass bodywork was easy to fit and any parts that readers of the book were unwilling to make themselves could be bought prefabricated from the factory. *How To Build Your Own Tiger Avon Sports Car For Road And Track* was underway and, following a deal with Veloce Publishing, had a large specialist publisher behind it to give it the mass market appeal Jim Dudley was after.

As we go to press, the Tiger Avon is just beginning to make an impression on the conventional kit car market, while the book to support it is due for launch imminently. While the Tiger Cat remains the company's core focus when it comes to conventional kit car marketing, Tiger is hugely excited about the prospects for the book-based Tiger Avon. Watch this space.

The factory car

We've driven a number of Tiger Cats over the years and the last was a factory-assembled example built specifically for a customer as one of the company's in-house turnkey cars. As it stood, the customer was paying out some £6800 and Tiger claims that if you built the car yourself you could do it for around £3500. The sums are easy enough – comprehensive Cat E1 kit at £3049 (inclusive VAT) plus donor kit package from Tiger at £411 equals £3460.

Not surprisingly, this customer had opted for one or two of the factory options over and above the standard Cat package. The side panels on the car were aluminium and would normally be left unpainted. In the cockpit there was a full compliment of instruments where normally you would only find a speedo and fuel gauge. It also featured Tiger's remote gear linkage which brings the gear lever closer to the driver. £4000? It doesn't sound far off, does it?

Under the bonnet was a reconditioned 2-litre Pinto with twin Weber carbs bolted on the side. Not monstrous power, but enough to give the Cat some entertaining performance.

The coloured gelcoat bodyshell is a standard Cat feature (and yes, you can mix and match colours for the wings, nose or any other panel that takes your fancy). Indeed, there aren't many extras available with the Cat. Apart from those taken up by this customer, he could have opted for adjustable seats, a full soft-top package, a chromed roll-over bar, 4-point harnesses and alloy wheels. Of course, in the engine and suspension department things can be as radical as your pocket dictates – rear disc brakes, vented fronts, 150bhp tuned Pinto, quickshift gearchange etc, etc.

As we've already established in the previous section, the Cat is almost exclusively Sierra based. Up front the donor's lower track control arm assembly is retained along with the stub axle. The original strut is binned and Tiger has reverted to an

Tiger Avon is the latest arrival at the factory. Spaceframe chassis is well sorted. Left: Avon looks the part. Below: Available as a kit from the factory or to build from scratch from a book.

in-board Spax coil-over damper arrangement with top rocking arm. At the back, Tiger has also opted for maximum use of the donor components, even retaining the Sierra subframe/De Dion tube affair. Four bolts take it off the donor car and simply the reverse it in place on the Tiger.

Back under the bonnet, Tiger uses its own specially fabricated radiator, a Cortina steering rack (supplied in the kit), a new master cylinder without servo. The steering column is from the donor, thus coming complete with column stalk controls, ignition switch and steering lock.

Finish on the test car was clean and tidy. The yellow gelcoat panels looked excellent, with all visible suspension components powder-coated along with the chassis. Inside the cockpit, Tiger's standard trim kit looked comprehensive, with only the simple seats perhaps hinting at a budget package. The company's adjustable seats would look more convincing, although they tend to take up a little more cockpit space, which was a deciding factor for this tall customer.

The existing seats weren't bad and we found the driving position comfortable and roomy. The centre tunnel is very high in the Cat, and it means that you use it as a natural armrest while flicking up and down through the gears. Production Cats have since reverted back to pendulum-mounted pedals but this car featured Tiger's own floor-mounted items that were well spaced and worked fine.

The stumpy gear lever made cog stirring quick and precise, and the optional remote linkage is a cheap option over leaving the lever in its standard position on the gearbox, where it exits quite far forward on the Cat centre tunnel, close to the dash. Out on the road the ride is very supple thanks to the Sierra's largely standard rear suspension, while Tiger's own front suspension arrangement is full of feel and delivers typically accurate steering inputs.

All in all, it was an accomplished performance that quickly reminded us that budget kit cars don't have to have economy levels of ride and handling.

The customer car

Affordability and a single donor car were key ingredients to Andrew Bridgman's choice when it came to building his first kit car. "I looked at Westfield," remembers Andrew, "and thought it was just too much money. I was looking at the Tiger and it was the right sort of money

Above: Most recent road test car was this factory built car for a customer. Below: Interior typically simple. High centre tunnel a dominating feature.

and with a single donor car." Having only recently jumped onto the career ladder, finances were tight and Tiger's projected £3500 build cost was as much as Andrew felt he could stretch to. As such, he ordered a basic Cat package, even to the point of not having the chassis powder-coated.

Having said that, Andrew did have the factory's standard trim kit and a host of other vital components to give him a head start when it came to assembling the car after his £35 donor Sierra had been stripped. Indeed, a long build time and developments at work allowed him to progressively upgrade the specification of the car, eventually buying alloy wheels and tyres through Tiger and sourcing a performance engine package from tuning expert, Vulcan Engineering.

"The build was OK," remembers Andrew, "but some of the manual wasn't very good and the photographs weren't very clear." Trickiest part of the whole assembly

Above: Andrew Bridgman has every reason to be pleased with his Tiger Cat. Built to a top spec, it not only looks the part but goes well too.

was when it came to the engine, which seemed an incredibly tight fit until Tiger recommended he cant it over slightly. Other problems included fitting the windscreen and sorting the floor-mounted pedals, which didn't seem to work terribly well.

Throughout any of these periods of head-scratching, Tiger proved excellent at offering advice over the phone and Andrew is full of praise for the company and its product. While the budget was originally tight, by the time he came to take the car for its SVA test he'd managed to relieve his bank account of some £6300 – way over our self-imposed budget of £5000. But we've let it stand in this case, because £1500 of that went on the Vulcan engine, an expensive upgrade that gives his car some serious performance.

If he'd retained the donor's engine, then it's easy to see what can be achieved when you use our budget on a top spec Tiger Cat. An optional full set of Tiger instruments sets the tone in the interior and, despite Andrew's retention of Tiger's basic seats, the Cat has an upmarket feel to it.

Fit and finish around the car is to a high standard, while features such as the stainless exhaust system are standard on even Tiger's most basic offering. Performance out on the road appears typically sharp and responsive, and Andrew's upgrade to a Vulcan engine obviously means this is a car that doesn't hang around for long.

Perhaps most encouraging to future Tiger Cat builders is the fact that Andrew feels it was easy to achieve such a high level of finish without making any special effort. Good news if this is your first kit car.

Chapter Seven
Blackjack Avion

The company

If Blackjack Cars seems a relatively new name to the kit car industry, its founder Richard Oakes is something of a walking, talking and designing icon. While a whole book could be given over to looking at the man and his automotive achievements over the years, one only has to mention cars such as the Nova, Midas Gold, GTM K3 and, most recently, GTM Libra to provide some idea of the talent we're talking about. When it comes to designing kit cars (and production cars) Richard Oakes knows his stuff.

But there's a world of difference between designing kit cars for your paying clients and deciding to manufacture and market your own product. While Richard has always been an extremely hands-on designer (more often than not making up the full size plugs from which production standard moulds can be made) he's only once previously decided to market a car, that being the Nova in 1972. So why the change in direction?

Below: Amazing GTM Spyder is Richard Oakes' most recent design for the kit car industry, with GTM having already commissioned the Libra, K3 and Rossa from Richard in the past.

Above: Iconic Nova was one of Richard Oakes first major success stories and, beyond the Blackjack, the only other car that he's designed and marketed.

"I wanted to bring about something which would eventually mean I could do something other than the design work," recalls Richard. "The design business has got lots of problems with it, in that it's a bit like being in the movie business – when you finish your frantic nine months of work, you finish up completely in a void. And because you've got your head down for this time you don't actually speculate on anything that might replace it. Any sort of good money you've earned disappears in the next three months while you're pitching for the next job. What's more, I always liked the customers when we were selling Novas."

Inspiration for the new car came in two forms. "I think three-wheelers have fascinated me for a long time but two things kicked it off. One was seeing the Liege when it was launched in about 1994. I remember thinking that it was the best thing there – it was just such a sweet thing. I'd already built this little mid-engined trials car thing and I'd got it sitting in my workshop and I wasn't really very pleased with

41

Richard Oakes (above) and his Citroën 2CV-based Blackjack Avion in action (below).

it – too many tubes, too complicated. When I saw the Liege at the show, I thought that it was just so much cleverer than what I'd done.

"Because the frame of the Liege is two-dimensional, there's no height to it – it's basically a three-point chassis like a Model T Ford – and because it's got this and there isn't much roll resistance, you can get away with this single plain chassis. I thought that was just such a neat way to make a chassis – back to basics in one sense but not an old fashioned chassis because it's all boxed so that it doesn't twist like old ones used to.

"The second thing to get me started was when Chris Rees's Three-Wheelers book came out in 1995. I thought that I'd like to do a three-wheeler and I wanted to do one with a frame like a Liege. I'd always liked the idea that three-wheelers are a perfect bit of engineering in the sense that they don't have the same twisting stresses [as a four-wheeler]. So as soon as you've got a three-wheeler you can start reducing everything because you don't need all that torsional stiffness. I just thought what a nice little niche to be in. Where you're really looking for about twenty-five nutters a year and you've got the entire world to look for them!"

Not surprisingly, Richard had clear ideas about what he wanted in the new car and, more importantly, what he didn't want. "At the time I thought I didn't want it to be like a Morgan or a Lomax although I could recognise that the 2CV stuff was pretty well perfect for doing the job. I didn't want it to be one of those things that you tend to rattle about in. I wanted it to be a much tighter thing than that...I thought it has to be something with no doors, it has to be a very minimal thing that just fits around two people. It has to be two because things that are one or three are just anti-social or a bit weird.

"But what I wanted was to do something more like some of those Thirties aerodynamic things – not like a replica but just with some of that aerodynamic styling. I looked inside little aeroplanes like Cessnas because I wanted to know what would be an acceptable space in which to put people. If you look in those things they're like an Austin Seven. In a sense, that kind of intimacy was sort of what I wanted to bring back because I think we've all got so used to sitting in big cars where you don't touch shoulders."

When it came to the donor car, Richard knew exactly what he was after. It was the Citroen 2VC. "There are no others," he says. "The bikes haven't got enough flywheel on them for a car. You are going to wear it all out so quickly and then you've got no reverse – just about everything about them is wrong really. I've nothing against those cars but it wasn't what I wanted to do."

There were also dynamic issues to consider. "To make a good three-wheeler it should be front-wheel-drive because you need the drive to go through two wheels." So, another nail in the bike engine argument.

While the 2CV engine was ideal for the new car, Richard wasn't about to retain its heavy platform chassis and he wasn't about to accept the Citroen's cataclysmic body roll through the bends. As such, a brand new lightweight, tubular ladderframe chassis soon materialised onto which the Citroen engine and front suspension swing arms could be bolted. However, the 2CV's longitudinally mounted spring arrangement was binned in favour of considerably more efficient vertically mounted coil-springs and separate dampers. Add in a stiffer anti-roll bar and you have a car that corners with superb body control.

Because the Blackjack's rear wheel is so visible (and also to reduce weight), a bespoke rear suspension arm with single coil-over damper unit replaces the original Citroen item used in some other three-wheelers.

To maintain strength in the body, the main fibreglass tub section can almost be described as a semi monocoque and onto this main section are added the hinging front bonnet and removable tail section. Of course, being the designer he is, Richard Oakes has also

Above: Despite having only one wheel at the back, the Blackjack performs beautifully. Below: 2CV engine is surprisingly potent.

ensured that the interior of the Blackjack is as impressively sculpted as the exterior – simplicity is the name of the game, but items such as the unique bench seat arrangement are a real feature in here.

With the project really coming to fruition, there was the minor issue of a name to find. "I'd had Blackjack on my mind for a long time," remembers Richard. "I can't tell you where it came from exactly but I always thought this was a great name. If you said it once to somebody they wouldn't forget it because it's kind of in your consciousness for some reason. It's got that nice sound to it. But it was wrong as a model name because the car was kind of airy and romantic and French and aircraft-like, so I couldn't quite reconcile that for a bit. But then I got a letter from somebody one morning and it said Par Avion on the top of the envelope, and I thought...that's the name. That's French for aeroplane – that's the name of the car!"

Above: Blackjack owner, Keith Pitt, stands behind Carol and Peter Pitts with their aero-screened Avion.

As the launch date drew closer Richard also needed to finalise his costings for the car and, while he always knew from the outset that the Blackjack Avion had to be competitively priced, the end product was proving costly to manufacture. "It all came out more expensive than I wanted it to. I wanted it to be something people could do quite cheaply but at the same time I was aware that if you built a Lomax Lambda, it was likely to cost six or seven thousand pounds. As I kept adding it up it kept coming to much the same figure."

As it happens, Richard doesn't feel that money has been a major stumbling block for his existing customers and he reckons the average build cost is between £5500 and £7000. Typically Richard finds that his customers will either buy about £2500 worth of kit bits and pieces initially or they'll order every last nut and bolt from the outset. However, he's increasingly finding that some customers are opting for just a basic chassis package to get them started.

Getting under our magic figure of £5000 isn't too much of a problem. "If I was doing a sub £5000 car," says Richard, "I'd want the wheels and I'd forgo other things but other people will use cheap wheels but have a hood and V-screen instead." Certainly, the spoked wheels are a huge part of the kit package, amounting to over £1000 by the time you add in tyres. But many customers have retained the original Citroen steel wheels, getting them bead-blasted and then repainted and the results can be surprisingly effective.

Looking back over the last five years of continuous production, becoming a manufacturer instead of a designer hasn't all been plain sailing. "I think the car is exactly what I had in mind but I've been disappointed with sales," observes Richard. "But we've also been in a changing market." But the Avion hasn't only had to battle against a changing marketplace. "Actually I think it [the bold design] was a mistake in a way because it took a long time for that to become acceptable. There were a few people who really liked it initially but most of the people were still looking for a Morgan replica."

Above: Keith's car features bucket seats and engine-turned dash panels while Peter's car has Blackjack's terrific bench seat.

44

Thankfully, today it's a different story. "I think people have got used to it now."

The factory car

While the styling of the Blackjack may have grown on some of Richard Oakes' customers, we've always loved the looks of this distinctive creation. There's not a bad angle on it and, whether you're looking at the interior or exterior, it's obvious that the car has been penned by a professional rather than simply an enthusiast.

The current red demo car has been on the road for a little while now and it's a well sorted package that we've experienced on a number of occasions. For our most recent encounter the car sported the company's new aero-scuttle, a bolt-on retro-fit option that replaces any of the Avion's existing screen options with a more enveloping fibreglass structure that includes tiny hinged doors. It transforms the look of the car, giving it a distinctly more modern and sporty feel while also offering increased protection from the elements. On balance, we probably prefer the car in its original form, as witnessed by the two customer cars in the next section, but as it's only a bolt-on option you could always chop and change as the mood takes you.

While the aero-scuttle doors swing up and away to give easy access to the interior, you really notice the

Alongside the factory car, with its new aero-scuttle, you can clearly see the different windscreen options.

difference once you're in. Not only does the scuttle section sweep right over the steering wheel, meaning that your hands are under it when driving, but the doors tuck in neatly around you to give a considerably more enclosed feeling than when sat in the conventional car. On longer runs Richard reports that this new arrangement makes the car considerably more comfortable.

The bench seat, which is a wonderfully sculpted affair that hinges forward to give access to the small rear boot space, is encouragingly comfortable while inertia reel seat belts are a welcome mod con. With two on board you'd better know your passenger pretty well since it's a snug fit. While the seat has no instantaneous adjustment, there is a facility for moving it into a number of different positions by unbolting the two hinge pins and simply slotting the bench into another locking point.

As it stands, the driving position is pretty good, while the dash-mounted gear change is close to the wheel and soon feels perfectly natural, if a little odd to start with because of its strange gate (first gear being left-and-back, second forward-and-centre and so on). Under the bonnet of this car the reconditioned engine has the addition of a twin carb set-up offering a healthy boost in power (standard being around 26bhp).

If you're the shy and retiring type, then the Blackjack really isn't for you since it attracts just as much, if not more, attention than any Cobra replica or outrageous supercar.

First impressions are certainly positive. The structure feels super rigid and suspension surprisingly supple. There's certainly no jarring ride here, which perhaps should not come as a surprise considering the donor's soporific ride quality. It's also immediately clear that any noticeable roll has been banished to the history books because the Avion corners eagerly and flat.

Less pleasing features include a distinctly limited turning circle (really very poor indeed), heavy-ish steering and a slow gearchange. However, when you really start giving the engine a serious caning the Avion's sports car capabilities really come to the fore. Push on several hundred revs beyond where you might think you should have gone and the tiny machine just keeps on going.

Above: Full screen and hood add quite considerably to the build costs. Peter and Carol retained the aero-screen that came with his part-built car.

Changes from second to third gear can be relatively quick and such is the gearing that third will easily see you hit sixty-five before you need to change up into top.

One surprise of the new aero scuttle is the increased effect of wind on your face. With the upswept perspex screen now considerably closer to you, there's less opportunity to sweep the air up and away, resulting in more wind around your head. Actual buffeting is reduced and there's probably no back draft at all, but this system certainly enforces the use of a decent pair of shades or goggles.

A much more welcome development is the reduction in buffeting inside the cockpit, which is vastly reduced when compared to the standard car. Here, the new set-up offers a marked improvement and will unquestionably make longer journeys more comfortable. At the national speed limit, the Avion actually feels surprisingly relaxed and with the right head-gear it would be quite possible to travel reasonable distances in comparative ease.

Grip through the skinny single rear tyre rarely seems to be a problem and for the most part you can simply forget that out back you're one wheel short. However, despite the skinny rubber, handling through the twisty bits is never a problem. The Avion always remains predictable and invariably surprisingly competent. Add in the solid feel of the whole structure and it's an encouraging performance.

As for the fun factor, the Avion is up with the very best in the industry. Great to look at, it sounds unlike anything else, has that quirky gear lever sprouting from the dash and is, of course, minus one rear wheel. But perhaps most surprising of all is the Avion's genuine drivability. It really is great fun to stoke up the engine and throw the car through the corners. But park up just about anywhere and the Avion is the instant centre of attention.

From a more technical stand-point, it's unlikely that an Avion build will test your skills too much. The simple chassis, tiny engine, single body tub and minimalistic interior should make this a straightforward and rewarding project, although you'll need to be quite careful in order to finish under our budget.

The customer cars

As has occurred on a number of occasions throughout the assembly of this book, we were fortunate enough to meet up with not one but two Blackjack customers. In this instance, one was built without recourse to a strict budget and shows what can be achieved when you can stretch your finances a little beyond our self-imposed budget, while the other was assembled for very little money indeed (around £3500). Peter Pitts (who came along with his wife Carol) was forced to opt for the second option and chose to buy an unfinished project off another Blackjack customer rather than build a car from scratch. Keith Pitt, on the other hand, dealt directly with the factory throughout and estimates his outlay at nearer £6000.

Buying projects that other people have either given up on, got bored with or simply no longer have the inclination to complete is often an exceptionally good way of getting a kit car project on the road very cheaply. The original outlay made by the primary customer is never reflected in the resale figure and yet often the first person has already sourced a lot of the donor components and may have spent out on engine upgrades, wheels and tyres and other components that quickly bump up the cost of a project. So a kit package that may have cost the original owner £10,000 may easily be on offer for little more than £4000 or less.

While both Blackjack customers may have approached their respective projects from different angles, they're both very much in agreement about the appeal of the Avion. "I saw an article on the car in the Daily Telegraph when Richard first brought it out," Keith comments, "and I was struck by it as soon as I saw it. It's just beautiful. The lines are perfect. It looks pretty where others look ugly – they might be interestingly ugly, but they're ugly. This to me is just stunningly beautiful." Peter is equally enthusiastic: "I consider the Avion to be a work of art. It's a living sculpture which I can get into and be a part of by building it."

Interestingly, neither man has built a kit car before and both went ahead with the build for similar reasons, beyond the basic appeal of the design. Neither would claim to be mechanically minded and the straightforward layout of the Avion was a winner. "What really appealed to me," explains Peter, "was the simplicity. When I looked in the engine bay of Richard's demonstrator I thought I could tackle it. When I looked at the other cars they looked complicated." Even so, Peter found the option of a part completed kit appealing. "I didn't feel that I was going to be capable of building a car from scratch, so when I saw one advertised in the classifieds I snapped it up."

While already assembled by its previous owner,

Blackjack's aero-scuttle is a recent addition to the car and can be retro-fitted when funds allow.

Peter's purchase was immediately stripped back to the bare chassis before being rebuilt to a standard that he was happy with. Having bought the car on Valentine's day 2001, it hit the road for the second time in mid-August of that year. Throughout both men's build projects, Richard Oakes was always on hand with help and advice. "I spent a lot of time on the telephone to Richard, who's extremely good," Keith enthuses. "He never makes you feel you're wasting his time."

While Peter's second-hand Blackjack came with the basic aero screen, Keith was after the added weather-protection of a full screen and soft-top. Having said that, fitting the screen wasn't without aggro. "The full screen introduces problems because you also have to have a windscreen wiper and, because you have the wiper, you have to have a windscreen wiper motor and that goes in behind the instrument panel and it takes up space where there isn't much space anyway." Keith's also the first to admit that the hood ruins the

Above: Built from an unfinished kit, Peter and Carol Pitts' car was completed for just £3500.

looks of the car when it's raised, but he keeps everything in place under a specially made hood cover and has resorted to its use on a number of occasions.

As we set the three cars up for the photo shoot it's easy to take in the three different wind deflecting options. Peter Pitts' car, with its Aston Martin metallic green finish, is perhaps the most aesthetically pleasing, although Keith's choice of a lovely Citroen white also suits the Avion to a tee and looks every part the classic car with its full screen treatment. With its rich red colour and the new aero scuttle, Richard's demo car unquestionably has the most modern and contemporary feel.

A quick run out in the two customer cars soon demonstrates the appeal of the Avion. Peter's basic aero-screened car works a treat, with a degree of buffeting, but the air being effectively swept up and over the occupants. Surprisingly, Keith's full screened example is much the same, without any great improvement or detriment. The screen is canted over at quite an angle and this almost certainly helps in keeping any buffeting to a minimum.

Peter Pitts sums it up perfectly. "This car is the greatest thing that you can have in the sense of the giggle factor. I drive a Mondeo for a 1000 miles a week in my job and when I come home I can have a blast in the Avion and people seem to smile and wave. It's nothing to do with how fast it is but it's the fact that you're having fun, and I love it because of that."

Chapter Eight

MK Indy

The company

MK Engineering is a no-frills kit car company. The small industrial unit is utterly devoted to chassis and suspension fabrication and, while there is an office of sorts, there's not enough room to swing a small rodent, let alone a furry animal of the feline variety. You'll also have a great view of the loo which, because space is tight, also seconds as an additional storeroom. So creature comforts are few and far between at MK, but one suspects that is just how MK MD Martin Keenan likes it to be.

Martin moved into this new unit in 2001 when demand became such that his home-based operation simply couldn't cope. Rolling chassis and full builds are still done at his house, while the fibreglass is the only part of the MK package that is farmed to outside contractors. But it was always the metal side of the work that made MK's name initially, and it's immediately obvious that the engineering side of the business is still where Martin Keenan gets his kicks.

"Before I was doing kit cars," recalls Martin, "I had a small engineering company doing general fabrication work, but my hobby has always been cars. Go karts, motorbikes, side cars, oval racers, stock cars – I've built and raced them all." But it was when Martin read Ron Champion's book, *Build Your Own Sports Car For As Little As £250*, that he built his first road-going car.

From the very outset he went his own way with

Born out of the Locost phenomenon, the MK Indy is now an independent product all on its own.

49

Martin Keenan is utterly focused on solid engineering and keeping things affordable – our sort of man.

certain aspects of the chassis and suspension design and it was the professional level of finish that got his car noticed. "I went to a few shows and people asked me to supply parts and then it went from one thing to another and I thought there might be a market for us." And he wasn't wrong!

Soon MK Engineering was busy manufacturing wishbones and full chassis for those enthusiasts who'd been bitten by the bug but didn't fancy welding up their own components. Interest was such that Martin then started supplying Ron Champion direct but it wasn't an arrangement that lasted long. Martin was quick to realise that the required Escort donor components were becoming increasingly thin on the ground and so he decided to do what every other Lotus Seven inspired manufacturer had already done – develop his own car based around Sierra components.

The MK Indy was the result, with a brand new chassis design utilising as much of the Sierra as possible. At the front it's a conventional twin wishbone affair currently using round tube upper wishbones and oval lower ones (oval tube upper wishbones in the pipeline). While the Sierra's stub axle is used, MK has devised a neat way of introducing some much needed geometry adjustment to the front end. "The mushroom inserts for the Sierra uprights [which fit into the stub axle top and locate onto the upper wishbone]," explains Martin, "are machined off-centre so that you can rotate them to change camber, castor and king pin inclination angles." It's a neat trick.

While he was sorting the front wishbones, he also decided to deal with the Sierra steering rack which, if used in unmodified form, would endow the car with unpleasant bump steer. By cutting the rack in half, shortening it and putting it back together again, MK has brought the pivot points for the steering arms into line with the suspension wishbones, thus ensuring that both suspension and steering components are moving in harmony rather than against each other (the conversion being done within the price of a basic kit).

At the back, the company initially developed a simple De Dion rear suspension system which uses the Sierra's differential, driveshafts and hubs but this has since been joined by a full IRS set-up with double wishbones and fabricated hub carriers on each side. "Some people prefer the De Dion," says Martin, "since it puts the power down better – for a race car it's quite good." But for the road little can beat the ride quality offered by a full IRS arrangement and the majority of current sales are for the latest system.

Another MK Engineering oddity is the option of either a wide track suspension system which retains the Sierra's

Below: Sierra-based MK Indy features a bespoke twin-wishbone rear IRS suspension system with MK's own fabricated uprights.

unmodified driveshafts (along with wide track wishbones at the front) or opting for a more conventional looking narrow track version. The two set-ups are available on both the De Dion and IRS chassis, the wider option keeping costs down slightly thanks to the lack of modification to the donor's driveshafts.

Having initially left Locost enthusiasts to find their own fibreglass panels, MK was quick to develop a basic set of wings and a nose cone for its own cars, and for the latest kits that's now been extended to a full set of self-coloured GRP panels, including the sides and bonnet. Even the dashboard is supplied in a leathergrain effect plastic which can be cut and moulded to a customer's own design. But before you think that the MK product is rapidly heading down the route of supplying endless options for seemingly peripheral items, the company still relies on its customers sorting out weather gear and other 'luxuries'.

What's more, the cars we were able to see on the day showed that the MK is still open to enormous interpretation by customers who often go their own way in order to keep costs to a minimum. Despite the company now operating in a conventional kit car manner (being able to supply every last nut and bolt required to build a car) the bare bones approach that has been the backbone of the company to date still stands true.

The factory car

MK's own demo car has been positively thrashed for the last 8000 miles and, despite its fantastic paint job, it's beginning to look tired. Martin certainly takes no prisoners when he's behind the wheel and happily

MK demo car has been well thrashed in its lifetime and the bike-engine has held up well.

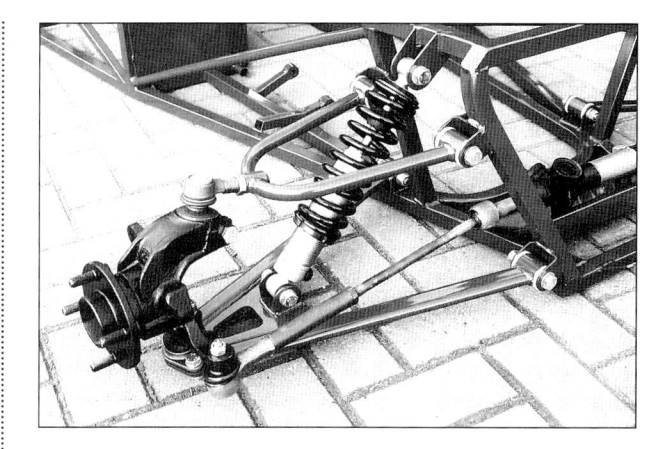

Sierra-based front suspension. Mushroom insert in the top of the Sierra stub axle is offset to allow a degree of camber and castor control.

performs a few doughnuts for us outside his unit – by all accounts it's a familiar display! His demonstrator isn't quite up to current specification, in that it retains the older De Dion suspension set-up and still has aluminium side panels where the current kits go out with an all-fibreglass package.

The test car features MK's own high-back seat shells and they're adequately comfortable and, thanks to runners, can be adjusted for a good driving position. On the move through the corners you can feel the seat back twisting a bit but not unduly. 4-point aircraft style harnesses (where each part clips into the central buckle separately) always work better than the more conventional 4-point harnesses, even if they do cost considerably more. Floor-mounted pedals are well spaced and the whole driving position is encouragingly positive from the outset.

Thanks to a quick steering rack, this car has an immediate and responsive steering action that encourages more spirited driving, although it's countered by being a little over-light and lacking the absolute level of feel that gives a driver complete confidence. Add in a slightly damp and cold winter's day with extremely slippery roads and minimal rear grip thanks to almost bald tyres (from all those doughnuts!) and it's not exactly an ideal test scenario.

The ride quality on this De Dion car is pretty good, although it is subsequently shown a clean pair of heels by the IRS customer car we drive later. Like many of MK's customers, this car has a Blade engine under the bonnet and

Bare fibreglass seat shells are all that's required in this stripped-out roadster.

careful selection of a suitable rear differential, along with larger 15" wheels endow it with near perfect gearing for fast road use. With loads of manic gearshifts through the sequential gearbox it is easy to settle at the ideal option for every corner.

If there's a downside to the bike fitment, then the lack of reverse can introduce problems. Despite the fitment of one of the most expensive aftermarket reverse boxes on the market (from 4-Wheel Motor Company at about £900) the transmission on this car is quite noisy and a bit

Two customer-built MKs, neither built for more than £3500 and one featuring a Fireblade bike engine – performance motoring doesn't get much cheaper.

Curved bulkhead chassis rails are a distinctive MK feature. Note engine subframe for a bike fitment.

clonky through the gears thanks to the extra cogs. It's a familiar trait when any reverse box is added into a bike transmission – the gear shift hardly being the most refined operation, even on its own.

So should you save the money and leave the reverse box out of the equation? For our brief sortie, we certainly made use of the reverse gear on a couple of occasions and having such an option takes out a degree of worry when compared with a car lacking its fitment. What's more, MK's Martin Keenan has some good news in this department. "I have an electric one coming out shortly for our cars," he comments, "with a variable speed controller on it and a lever to throw it in and out. It'll be cheaper than anybody else's and it really works. However, it'll only work on a car with a fixed diff because it mounts on the propshaft flange."

Of course, performance is the main reason for choosing a bike engine and the MK demo car doesn't disappoint. With its optional lightweight chassis, this car makes the most of the bike's 135bhp and there's no question that acceleration is anything short of electrifying. Add in the noise, stratospheric revs and seriously cool sequential gearshift and it's an intoxicating mix that has no comparison in the conventional car engine world – little wonder these units have become so fantastically popular.

But while the bike installation makes this MK hugely entertaining, Martin is the first to admit that such a fitment won't suit everybody. While virtually all his sales were for bike engined cars early on, now he reckons it's nearer 50:50, with many customers sticking with the 2-litre Pinto lump that comes free with the donor. There's little question that the bike option is certainly less practical, even for a car which is used only occasionally, so making the decision to go down this route shouldn't be taken lightly.

But take the Blade installation out of the MK and you're still left with an entertaining and extremely good value package. If you're on a genuinely tight budget, and by that we mean sub £4000, then it's absolutely clear that the MK offers you a number of suspension options, all of which can be built to a good standard for the money. And the last part of the previous sentence is what really counts here, because it's always possible to build a kit car for next to nothing, but to build a decent kit car on a tight budget is quite a different matter.

What's more, it's not just the car we like – there's an infectious enthusiasm here for producing a good, honest product at an affordable price. There's no bluff and bluster, just down-to-earth good humour backed up by a solid product.

Top: Paul Verity had a very tight budget when he began his car and, all in, it won't have cost him more than £2000 to complete. Below: Donor Pinto engine should give solid performance.

The customer cars

Not surprisingly, most MKs are built on a tight budget and we weren't exactly short of potential cars to feature for this section of the chapter. Paul Verity's white car runs a De Dion rear suspension set-up and was put together for just under £2000. Andy Mullin's yellow example runs the later IRS rear suspension package and he reckons his car has cost him nearer £3500. On the basis that it's got a mental Honda Fireblade engine under the bonnet you begin to appreciate just what fantastic value for money these cars represent.

As a trained mechanic, Paul Verity wasn't too worried about a back-to-basics kit car project but he was rather more concerned about his budget which, from the outset, wasn't a lot! As with a few other owners we've looked at in this book, Paul was fortunate enough to get his hands on a second-hand MK chassis, and buying any unfinished project can be a great way of saving some money. Being very local to MK's workshop has also played its part, because he's been able to pop round and have a look at completed cars whenever he's needed some additional advice or inspiration.

"I've had a lot of help from friends who I've done favours for," says Paul, "so I've really kept the cost down." As such, servicing the car of a guy who does car upholstery means he's got some natty seat covers for the MK fibreglass buckets. Much the same can be said for

Below: Paul Verity's car features MK's De Dion rear suspension option.

the flashy bits of chrome on his car – so a healthy bit of bartering is alive and well in the bargain basement world of economy kit cars.

Indeed, Paul's ingenious cost saving exercises have also seen him use Citroen 2CV front headlights, motorbike coil-over dampers for the front suspension and Mini rear dampers with over springs for the back. Not surprisingly, Paul also made his own wiring loom and, when it came to the aero screen, cut out the perspex himself. "I went for the old fashioned look," he comments. "I didn't want something straight so I put a bit of a curve in it."

Thinking about his engine options, Paul quickly

Right: Andy Mullin was looking for some extreme performance from his MK, hence the Fireblade bike engine (below) – end result still didn't cost him more than £3500.

Right: Extensive bartering has helped to keep the build cost down on Paul Verity's car – servicing the trimmer's daily runabout got these great seat covers. Above: Instruments came free with donor.

discounted any thought of a bike installation. "I like a little bit more useable power, a nice torquey engine – so the bike engine is a bit too track-day-ish." Using the 2-litre Pinto engine that came with the donor car, the injection system was dumped and a single twin-choke Weber bolted on in its place. The height of the Ford block means he's had to cut a hole in the top of the bonnet to gain enough clearance, but MK tells us that newer chassis have an inch of extra height in them which does away with the need to make any bodywork mods.

Paul's car wasn't quite on the road when we visited, with just a handful of items still to be fitted and SVA to overcome. Conversely, Andy Mullin's yellow car has been in regular use since it hit the road in September 2001. "I was into bikes for many years," he remembers, "but just decided they were getting too fast for me. I ended up selling my bike in 2000 and I bought a 1989 Westfield chassis which I panelled. Then somebody offered me some money for it so I sold it." Having looked around the various kit car shows, he was really taken by the MK chassis – in particular, the distinctive curved footwell treatment.

Working from a tiny single garage with a swing-up bench that was erected when Andy pushed the rolling chassis far enough out, it was always going to be something of a test to build the MK, but in just four months the car was complete!

Andy went for MK's fully independent rear suspension car and quickly found his original £2500 budget getting hammered as he opted for more expensive items such as MK's recommended coil-over dampers and, most significantly, a Honda Fireblade motorbike engine and gearbox. All in, he reckons the MK has now cost him around £3500.

Essentially, SVA was passed at his first attempt, the examiner failing the car on a couple of minor items which he was able to rectify on site and have an almost immediate retest. After that, he quickly heaped on about 1500 miles in the space of just three months, which is no mean feat in a bike-powered car. However, despite his love of the motorbike installation, he already knows that if he were to build another MK (a very likely outcome) then that car would have a Pinto engine in it. While the Blade lump is an awesome performer, its limited practicality is already beginning to tell.

With two on board, the IRS suspension is super compliant and, with MK's recommended Dampertech dampers on each corner, the car remains composed and feels well sorted. Performance from the Fireblade engine is as crazy as we've come to expect from these bike units but the selection of a very low geared rear differential made the first four gears largely irrelevant. That's a great shame when half the fun of a bike installation is zipping up and down the 6-speed sequential gearbox. Andy's aware of the problem and will be pulling out the diff over the winter and replacing it with something more suitable.

What was noticeable in his car was how quiet and smooth the gear changes were. He's not fitted with a reverse gearbox (which also helped to seriously reduce his outlay) and the lack of those extra cogs in the

Above: Andy's car also features MK's full IRS rear suspension system, for a surprisingly smooth ride on such a race-inspired hell-raiser.

transmission makes quite a difference. This is one of the smoothest and most refined set-ups we've come across and Andy swears that the lack of a reverse is no problem whatsoever.

The fit and finish around Andy's car is pretty good and indeed both customer-built examples of the MK have been carefully assembled by their respective builders. However, neither car is what we'd describe as immaculate and, despite Andy's having been on the road for several months, neither car is actually 'finished' – although that's a word you have to be very careful about using when describing any kit car! There's always more to do and things which are in the midst of being changed or updated.

The final finishing touches will come in due course but what these two cars very clearly demonstrate is that it is genuinely possible to build an MK on an extremely tight budget and, in the case of the bike-engined car, even when using serious performance parts. At just £3500 we doubt there's much in the kit car world to touch it.

Chapter Nine

Fisher Fury Spyder

The company

You can't run a successful kit car operation without working hard at it and there are certain companies within the kit car scene which always appear to be particularly focused – Fisher Sportscars is most certainly in this latter group. Main man at the company is Mark Fisher and it's pretty fair to say that he has worked his socks off over the last decade to ensure that Fisher Sportscars has not only become, but has remained, one of the most successful operations at the upper end of the kit car midfield.

While there's little doubt that the Fury is one of the prettiest roadsters on the market, and therefore sells itself to a degree, it's the company's dogged determination and enthusiasm for the product that has ensured sales figures that are almost certainly on the healthy side of good. But being a kit car manufacturer was not always paramount in Mark Fisher's mind...

As a professional specialist model maker, doing everything from architectural mock-ups to advertising

Fisher Fury Spyder is where we're at, although building a standard Fury shouldn't cost a great deal more.

Above: Full TUV Approval opened up markets in Europe via Fisher's continental agents.

props, he always made time for his hobby – cars. "I'd had Caterhams and Duttons and modified them extensively and really got into the scene," remembers Mark. "I nearly bought a Sylva Leader at the time when Jeremy [Phillips of Sylva Autokits] was first starting to race the new Striker. I ended-up buying a Mk3 Striker when I already owned a BDA Caterham."

A move from being an employee in London to setting up his own model making company in Kent was unfortunately timed to coincide with the early onset of the Nineties recession, and it quickly hit home. At much the same time, Mark found his enthusiasm for kit cars was beginning to rub off on others – people were coming to him asking if he could either build them a car from scratch or finish off a project on which they'd given up.

With his enthusiasm for the Sylva marque, Mark began to wonder whether the kit car world might offer an invaluable buffer while his model-making business fought off the recession. Appointed as Sylva's southern

Above: Hard-top just one of many developments done by Fisher over the years.

agent in 1991, the newly launched Fisher Sportscars went for it big-time. Mark was especially keen on Sylva's newest model, the Fury, and the company was soon making a name for itself. "We were putting a lot of effort into selling kits, going to all the shows, and we ended up selling a lot of Furys."

By 1993, the ever-productive mind of Sylva's Jeremy Phillips was looking to move on from the Fury to develop the next project (which would become the Stylus) and it seemed quite logical to offer the production rights of the existing car to Fisher. Mark didn't need to be asked twice. "We put a huge effort into marketing it," recalls Mark, "particularly abroad, because at that time the pound was very weak and that was when the German agent was very keen to put it through TUV, so we helped them with that. At that time we were also selling cars in Belgium, Japan, all over the place." Fisher Sportscars continues to work closely with Sylva Autokits and remains its southern agent to this day.

Development of the Escort-based Fury began almost immediately. The Japanese were after an IRS based car and Jeremy Phillips helped develop the first of three different independent rear suspension systems. The latest of these uses a very similar version of Sylva's Striker IRS arrangement, with double wishbones each side, fabricated uprights and a Sierra differential.

The competition side of Fisher's business has always been significant, and the Fury was soon offered with a lightweight chassis and new Spyder rear bodywork which lacked the doors found on the standard car. Indeed, Fisher's competition interests are even stronger today, especially with the launch of a dedicated bike-engined race series which has proved especially popular with his customers. One of the more recent developments here is the use of a Land Rover Freelander rear differential and driveshafts, which offer considerable weight savings over the conventional Sierra components.

If the mechanical side of the car has been

Racing involvement has always been central to Fisher marketing over the last ten years.

continually tweaked, the bodyshell has also been developed over the years. "We actually offer three different types of bonnet now," Mark explains. "The original one which we call the Classic, then the Big

Mark Fisher is the man behind the company and he's worked ceaselessly to ensure the operation has been a big success.

Above: The company has always offered a full or part-build-up service. Left: Factory Open Day always well supported.

Bulge one which takes most engine options and finally we brought out the Le Mans bonnet which has got higher wings and Perspex light covers. With SVA coming out in 1997, headlight heights on the original bonnet were a concern of ours. We were involved with the SVA pilot scheme, submitting a car to one of the London SVA stations for them to assess before SVA came out.

"This was after we had done the Le Mans bonnet and we took a car along with the Big Bulge bonnet and it was fine. That was because they measure to the dipped beam cut off line on the lens and not to the bottom of the headlight, as we'd previously assumed. That made a tremendous difference."

The onset of SVA hasn't affected the car too badly, with minor alterations required to the way the bonnet is fastened, a few internal edges being more rounded and the seat belt mounting points being moved (ironically, from the position in which they passed German TUV!). Like many manufacturers, Fisher Sportscars has become something of an expert on the subject and offers both a pre-SVA check for its customers and also a full SVA service where the company will take the car to the test and undertake any corrections that may be required in order for the car to pass. Not only popular with existing Fury customers, the company is finding that many local kit car enthusiasts are taking up the offer with their own non-Fisher kits.

While kit sales are the mainstay of the business, Fisher has always been involved in partial and full builds for customers both in the UK and abroad. By the mid-Nineties it had hit something of a peak. "We did thirty or forty built cars for Belgium and they were a mix of Strikers and Furys. We were literally building two Strikers a month," says Mark. "We had a team of guys who were just putting cars together. Now we probably do one a month. Often they're to a basic stage to get through SVA and then the customer takes them away to do the trimming etc.

"We've changed our business since then because we've reassessed what we want to do. It comes down to the fact that we're enthusiasts about the cars. Our

Below: Just about any engine will fit the Fury, as witnessed by this very tidy Rover V8 installation. Below right: Modern Ford Zetec a very popular, but expensive, fitment.

Above: Simple Ford X-flow in the company demo car is where savings can be made (although twin carbs up the ante somewhat!).

core business is the kits and we'll do builds – but only the ones we want to do. We used to have four or five guys here and, while your turnover goes up, the profits don't."

Today it's not only the number of full builds that has changed – the whole market has moved on. "What we're finding is that more and more customers just want a toy – instead of having a motorbike in the garage they've got a kit car and they only use it on fine days," observes Mark. "We currently sell slightly more Spyders than ordinary cars – I think that's a trend because we're moving more into the racing side. I think it will also swing more over to IRS because of lack of availability with the Escort bits."

And while the basic kit price has altered little since Mark took on the Fury project almost ten years ago, he knows full well that the finished cars are invariably costing their owners considerably more. "People now fit Zetecs and K-Series engines and the price of these units is a lot more than people used to spend. 75% of our customers buy their donor parts fully reconditioned from us whereas ten years ago the majority of people were buying a donor car and doing it all themselves – rebuilding their own engines etc."

If there's a downside to these high-spec creations, it is that they can lead to the perception that the core product has also gone up in price and Mark's adamant that a Fury can still be built on a budget. "Most of our customers fall into the £6000-£8000 mark," he explains, "but to build a car more cheaply people have got to concentrate their minds on getting the bits at the right prices. They might get a second-hand set of wheels or use the donor ones." While there's little difference in price between the Spyder shell and conventional Fury, other big savings will come from using the donor's Pinto or X-flow engine and perhaps even retaining the original instrument binnacle instead of buying an expensive set of aftermarket gauges.

A visit to Fisher Sportscars' compact unit on a pretty

Above: Simple Fury Spyder demo car has been used harder than most – initial driving impressions show it's extremely well sorted. Below: Rally inspired dash design isn't for show.

Kent industrial estate will invariably be an enlightening experience. Hundreds of photographs pinned to the walls have been sent in by their enthusiastic owners and aptly demonstrate the diversity of finishes that can be achieved. With two demonstrators available on our visit (one a budget car and the other a bike-engined, high-spec blaster) and other cars in mid-build and with kits awaiting collection, there's loads to see. What's more, a quick run out in either of the test cars should quickly show you why the Fury has become one of the most popular roadsters on the market.

The factory car

Practising what he preaches, several years ago Mark Fisher set about building a Fisher Fury Spyder on a tight budget and, some four years later, the car is still in the

59

Top right: Drinks bottles are an odd engine bay feature but carry spare oil and water for when the car's being used in rallies. Storage space also vital for these longer jaunts.

factory showroom. Having covered an amazing 25,000 miles in no fewer than three European rallies has certainly given this car a tougher life than most, but it more than proves you don't need to go high-tech to be effective.

The specification for this Fury is ultra straightforward. While there's little difference in kit price between the standard car and Spyder option, the latter's lack of a windscreen or doors means you can forgo windscreen wipers, heater, door hinges and release catches plus a few other more minor sundries – these may not cost the earth, but their removal certainly makes the build more straightforward. But of

Fisher was one of the first companies to embrace the bike-engine phenomenon that has swept the kit car scene in the last few years.

more significance is the use of a simple Escort live axle in place of the more modern (and more expensive) IRS. Up front you'll find that faithful old campaigner, the Ford X-flow, instead of any fancy twin-cam 16-valve whiz-bang modern lump. Add in a simple aluminium dash, an almost complete lack of interior carpeting and basic fibreglass seat shells and you have a recipe for a very cheap kit car.

As you've already read in the previous section, Fisher Sportscars offers a bewildering number of different body options. The demonstrator features the company's Le Mans bonnet with optional headlight 'eyelashes' instead of Perspex covers. The Spyder rear body section obviously means a lack of doors, but this car also features the company's optional flared rear arches, largely designed to accommodate larger wheel/tyre combinations for the race cars.

While this demonstrator wasn't originally conceived as a rally car, a quick glance inside immediately sets the tone. The stark dashboard has the usual gaggle of instruments while items such as a cigarette lighter socket, clock and map light hint at its more purposeful life. Finally, tucked away in front of the passenger seat is a Brantz Rally meter for accurate section timing, average speed calibration etc.

Under the bonnet it's all pretty familiar stuff – a tidily presented X-flow looks the part thanks to some fat twin Webers and shiny stainless steel exhaust. Up front a whopping radiator gives a clue to the desert destinations that this car has had to cope with, while the front sill on the driver's side has been converted into additional storage space. Two water bottles are mysteriously located down one side of the engine bay and further investigation reveals one is full of engine oil while the other has nothing more exciting than water – two vital components for long distance rallying in less than perfect driving conditions.

Apart from these largely cosmetic competition additions, this remains a very humble road specification car, but its years of serious road use are immediately apparent from the moment you drive away. While freezing conditions on the day of our visit precluded any serious driving, previous outings in this very car have always reminded us why the Fury remains such a popular kit.

The driving position is pretty much perfect, and while Fisher's fibreglass seat shells are a bit uncomfortable without any additional padding, they're perfectly accommodating with just a basic foam insert. Despite larger than standard 205x60 tyres, the steering remains light and yet full of feel. The turn-in is precise and the steering rack is the standard Escort item, not an expensive quick-rack unit.

Like the steering, the handling is light yet hugely confidence inspiring; the car has a flickability and predictability that mesh together to make a hugely competent road car. With standard front disc brakes and rear drums, even the braking is well up to scratch yet not dependent on expensive upgrades.

Under the bonnet the nicely tuned 1700cc X-flow should be developing around 130bhp and, while a rebuild to this specification doesn't come cheap, you'd be surprised how eager a more standard unit is with the simple addition of a twin-choke single carb. Alternatively, don't ignore the Sierra's 2-litre Pinto – cheap-as-chips down at your local scrappy, while the extra capacity comes with a free helping of torque for additional grin factor. Finally, don't discount the fact that you can always start with a standard engine to get you on the road and, when funds allow, move up to a tuned version.

As it stands, this tiny Fury is a startling performer, with electrifying performance and a 5-speed Sierra gearbox for long-legged touring ability. The success of the package is clear for all to see – a gold medal winner in the 5000-mile 1997 Liege-Agadir-Liege rally, repeated in the 4500-mile 1999 Liege-Targa-Liege event (plus team trophy) and, most recently, a silver medal winner in the 3000-mile Liege-Corse event. Tests of a car's ability don't get much tougher than this and speak volumes for the diminutive Fury's capabilities.

While money has been spent on the car since, Mark Fisher feels sure that its original build budget would have been within our £5000 benchmark. The fact that it has covered such a distance in relative ease and, most importantly, has been held onto by the manufacturer when he could have easily built a higher spec example, more than proves its worth.

The customer car

"I didn't have a load of money to spare," recalls Fisher Fury owner Dave Reed, "so I kept the budget as low as possible but with the emphasis on trying to get everything looking neat and tidy and all fitting together well. I didn't have a ceiling figure because I wasn't worried about the time it took me to build the car as the job could be extended over some time." In the end he took two years over the construction of his Fury and reckons the car set him back around £4800 all-in.

While Dave hasn't ever built a kit car before, he certainly knows one end of a spanner from the other.

Dave Reed built his car with a limited budget and managed to keep everything down to an impressive £4800.

Above: Twin-carb 1600cc engine offers solid performance in the lightweight Fury. Above right: Interior ultra simple and fuss-free.

"When I was about twenty I bought an E93A chassis off a mate with a side-valve engine on it and I found a fibreglass Falcon bodyshell and started to chop it about to make it fit. But it wasn't designed for that chassis so I started it but never finished." Later on he got into grass-track racing old Minis but a serious accident put him off that one and his automotive enthusiasm wasn't fired up again until he visited his local kit car show at Chatham in Kent. "I wandered around and had a look at the cars – the wife didn't complain too much so away we went!"

Not surprisingly, Dave's standard-bodied Fury features an Escort live back axle and Ford X-flow under the bonnet. Initially just a standard 1600cc GT unit, it's since been upgraded and, more recently, was replaced altogether for a considerably higher spec engine pumping out a handy 118bhp at the rear wheels. Of course, upgrading your car after you've built it means you can keep the costs down initially, get the car on the road and start enjoying it before you spend a bit more money on tuning goodies.

Just as the engine has developed over the years, so the gearbox has changed from a standard Escort 4-speed unit to a Sierra 5-speed 'box, and the result has been dramatic. "It transforms the car," says Dave. "It's much better for touring." And you can take him at his word, the car having been all over the UK and down through Germany. Throw in some track days for good measure and the occasional blast up a quarter-mile drag strip and it's clear Dave's certainly making the most of his car.

Looking around the Fury, which is now several years old, it's easy to see that this is a really good 'working' kit car. The engine bay is neat and tidy, the bodywork fits well and the interior has an encouragingly weathered look to it – one suspects that the mechanical side of the car is meticulously maintained while everything else takes second place. It's a car for using rather than endlessly polishing.

Future upgrades include revamping the simple dashboard, but items such as the minimalistic carpeting aren't a priority, with the original material being bought from a kit car show for just £5! However, there are bigger plans for under the bonnet. "I've been toying with the idea of modifying the X-flow," muses Dave, "by putting a steel bottom end in it but I've since gone off that idea so I'm now playing around with perhaps supercharging it." Now that would be interesting.

Looking back he's sure that he could have saved money. "I made a few mistakes in things that I bought. I think the most important thing when you're building a kit is planning – planning what you're going to use, doing lots of research and ensuring that you only buy once for something. See what other people have done first of all." Not that Dave is disappointed with his car – far from it, and he's already busily planning his trips for this year, including another trip to the Nurburgring and further track days in the UK. All this, and giving his son a helping hand with his Sylva Striker! There's no stopping some people.

Chapter Ten
Robin Hood

The company

If we're seriously talking about affordable kit cars then it is simply impossible not to include Robin Hood Engineering within this book. The company has, almost single-handedly, championed the cause for budget blasters over the last decade. In doing so, it has often infuriated its competition and been on the receiving end of some pretty fierce criticism.

But with the more recent onset of the Locost phenomenon and a number of other Lotus Seven inspired kit car manufacturers joining the budget end of the marketplace, perhaps everyone is beginning to understand what Robin Hood has been doing all these years. Put simply, it has been giving the public what it has always wanted – more affordable kit cars.

Indeed, keeping things cheap has always been the philosophy of Robin Hood MD, Richard Stewart. "I've been in the motor trade all my life, starting off doing domestic motor body repairs – you bend 'em, we mend 'em," he remembers. "We've always been really busy,

Robin Hood didn't always produce cheap kit cars. Its Daytona replica became more expensive as customers demanded ever higher standards of detailing.

Richard Stewart is the imaginative mind behind Robin Hood Engineering.

simply because we've always gone for value for money."

Richard Stewart Motor Body Repairs became well known in the Nottingham area, and Richard built on this notoriety by building a number of interesting one-offs, from a 6-wheeled Escort pick-up to Jaguar-based Ford Anglia!

"I really wanted to do something a bit more exotic but in Nottingham there wasn't that scope. So anything that I did, I had to finance myself. That's where the Robin Hood Daytona came into it. I took a Rover SD1, which had shades of Daytona about it, and did a replica for myself and it created a lot of interest.

"The first car I did was from pictures I'd seen in books. A journalist wanted to do a feature on it and he somehow persuaded a garage to let him have a real car. So we had the two cars together – it was quite sensational because I'd never seen one before and as soon as I'd seen one I realised there were one or two areas where we'd gone wrong. But he gave it a terrific write-up and from that I realised there was potential in it for production."

Left: First Lotus Seven inspired Robin Hood was this Triumph TR7-based creation, complete with 2-litre Triumph engine.

In the late Seventies, when the first Daytona came to life, Richard was dead set against the idea of kit cars and the SD1-based creations were a complex conversion. "We cut them into three," explains Richard, "extended the engine compartment and took away all the area behind you where the rear seats were. There was no fibreglass in it. We were heavily into classic restoration and we were already making steel panels for cars when they couldn't be bought – so we were already making panels on the wheeling machine."

With the potential for volume production on the new car, Richard dropped his repair business at the first opportunity. "As with everything I do, I woke up one morning and knew I'd had enough of doing body repairs – I don't want to do it anymore." That meant Richard needed a new name for the company, and its original premises in Sherwood, Nottingham, provided the inspiration. "Robin Hood Engineering was a name we thought of just like that, and we didn't realise what a powerful name it would be because it doesn't matter where you go in the world, everybody knows about Robin Hood."

With the Robin Hood instantly a big hit, bulk manufacture was the order of the day, even from early on. Car at this stage was still a spaceframe.

As the classic car market began to go into outer orbit, so people's interest in a more affordable replica grew, but the specification had to be spot-on. Rover V8 engines were soon replaced with Jaguar V12s and the standard of interior detailing was meticulous. By the mid-Eighties it was all getting a bit out of hand. "People were having to spend £25,000 for the package that we would give them, which wasn't a complete car – it would be a car ready for painting," recalls Richard. "I felt then that we were quite exposed and that we only needed the market to change slightly and we'd have two or three of the cars left with us."

A move to cheaper Triumph TR7 donor cars addressed the problem to a degree but Richard could smell trouble coming from across the pond in the States. "The Daytona had become popular because of the Miami Vice TV series where they were using a McBurnie Corvette-based replica. At the time there was a major problem in the States with imitation Rolex watches, and a firm of lawyers over there was very successful at getting this stopped. After the success with the watches, they went along to Ferrari and offered to do the same thing for them with the Daytona.

"This obviously made people in the UK a bit nervous and we looked very carefully at what we were doing. We spent a lot of money finding out whether we were open to any litigation, so we knew an awful lot about what you could and couldn't do with regards to copyright laws." While Robin Hood never fell foul of the roving American legal eagles, the information they'd amassed regarding copyright proved to be the trigger for the company's next project.

Still keen to get out of the Daytona market, Richard Stewart was looking for a new direction and a legal battle between Westfield and Caterham caught his eye.

Continued on page 81

Right: Andrew Bridgman has built a superb example of the Tiger Cat. Vulcan engine blew the budget, but otherwise this was an affordable kit car.

Left: Peter Pitts and his wife Carol bought their Blackjack Avion as an unfinished project and completed it on a tight budget while Keith Pitt (behind) worked without any significant cost restraints. Both cars are superb.

66

Right: Andy Mullin was determined that his MK Indy would have a bike engine while Paul Verity (bottom) was more than happy with the donor's Pinto block. Both cars were completed for under £3500 each!

Fisher's Mark Fisher gives the company demo a quick thrash. Dave Reed built his green example (below) for under £5000.

Reg Bridgman (right) completed his Robin Hood 2B for under £3500 and to standard factory spec.

Jim Brown is thrilled to bits with his immaculate JAS Buggy. Using largely new parts throughout lifted the build cost to around £4500.

70

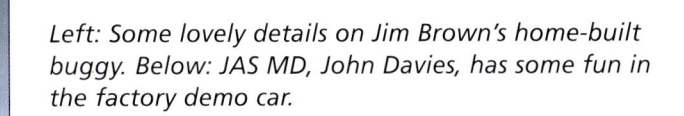

Left: Some lovely details on Jim Brown's home-built buggy. Below: JAS MD, John Davies, has some fun in the factory demo car.

Below: Jim Luke (foreground) and Keith Kirk (behind) built their Locosts together. Neither car cost more than £2000! Above: Engine bay neat and tidy and standard 1300cc Ford X-flow can easily be upgraded later.

Above: Dave Reed uses his Banham X21 everyday to get to and from work. 1100cc engine is cheaper to run and service than more popular 1400cc twin-cam.

Tempest is one of the very few traditionally styled kit cars that can be built within our budget.

Sylva Striker will stretch our finances, but it can be done.

Left: John Goodhand provided the factory with a lot of information regarding using a bike engine thanks to his autograss experience. Then he built himself this Suzuki Bandit-engined example.

76

MORE BUDGET BLASTERS...

Top: Vindicator Sprint is a quirky alternative to more conventionally styled machines such as the Stuart Taylor Locoblade (right). Below: Deauville Canard one of the few traditional roadsters within our budget.

Top: Marlin Sportster is a surprise entry in Budget Blasters. BMW donor helps to bring it within our budget. Left: Lomax 223 a long time favourite with budget builders. Lower left: Falcon LX3 a quirky alternative. Below: Renault 5-based Free Spirit still looks imaginatively styled.

Top: Slick Midas Gold Convertible is well worth consideration. Left: Banham Sprint is a Mini-based body conversion. Below: Autotune Gemini has been around for years and still represents great value for money.

Onyx Bobcat is a wacky Metro-based budget blaster.

NCF Blitz is superb off-road fun and literally dirt cheap.

Continued from page 64

Caterham wasn't too keen on the Lotus Seven inspired replica that Westfield was producing at the time and the ensuing legal battle resulted in Westfield halting production of the model now commonly referred to as a Pre-Litigation Westfield and launching its all-fibreglass SE.

It was a move which puzzled Robin Hood. "Armed with the information we'd got in order to keep our nose clean with Ferrari, we couldn't understand why Westfield had to stop what they were doing. Everybody was scared stiff to do anything, so we'd got the market to ourselves."

With a yard full of old TR7s, it was obvious which donor Robin Hood should use for its first attempt at a Lotus Seven inspired replica. Launched at the Stoneleigh kit car show in 1989, the RS TR7 was an immediate hit. "Cost was important because we were coming in at a sub Westfield price," recalls Richard. "There were people at that stage who wanted a Westfield but couldn't afford one. But they didn't want a Dutton because that was beginning to get a bad name, so they came to Robin Hood. The kit that we offered then is the identical same price as the new kit costs today and that's amazing."

While undercutting the opposition has an obvious advantage, there were other reasons why Robin Hood felt it was important to keep the price down. "One of the problems you've got with business in any form is keeping ahead of bad debts. If you can produce something where finance isn't involved and people can pay you for what they get, then you can afford to do your costings and trim the price of your product right down to the bone because you haven't got to incorporate any kind of loss. I knew that if we were going to sell a kit at £1000 or £1500, that was the kind of money that people had available."

While these first cars were based around a spaceframe chassis, Robin Hood was already working with the stainless steel panels that have since set the company's cars apart from any opposition. Kits were supplied with

Above: Monocoque design set Robin Hood apart from its rivals for much of the Nineties. Available in either mild steel or shiny stainless as an option.

stainless side panels already pre-fitted but the chassis, with all the tubes to be welded, was a time-consuming job that didn't lend itself to offering an affordable end product. "We realised that it was very difficult to get a spaceframe and clad it in metal within a relatively short time, so that's why we looked at a monocoque."

Combined with a move to cheaper Dolomite donor components, Robin Hood launched its first stainless steel monocoque chassis and quickly realised that ease of production wasn't the only benefit. "We were hearing all the time that people wanted more room than was available in a Westfield or Caterham and our cars were always wider. Without the tubes inside the cockpit there was once again a lot more room."

While the Triumph-based kit proved popular, a move to Ford components was inevitable and over the years the Robin Hood moved from Cortina to Sierra. But there was trouble ahead. Despite its advisers' confident assurances to

Right: Barrel-backed S6 was one of Robin Hood's less successful ventures while monster Jaguar V12-powered example was about as extreme as you could go!

Above: Bulk despatch days are another Robin Hood oddity. Kit designed so that it's easy to load onto a trailer or into a van.

the contrary, by 1994 Robin Hood found itself on the receiving end of a Caterham legal challenge, involving the use of the numeral '7' for its latest Sierra-based model.

Like other manufacturers before it, Robin Hood was also eventually forced to toe the line and each new model since then has had a different name, such as Exmo and 2B (a play on its new tubular chassis – "tubey"). As you'll see in the next section, the company's latest innovative model is named the Sub K (for fairly obvious reasons).

In 1992 it was time for one of Robin Hood's regular model reshuffles, and a chance visit to an autojumble at Newark was to have significant repercussions. "One of the key ingredients to this type of car is the fact that it has an exposed, attractive manifold that comes out of the side of the body," observes Richard, "and we went to Newark one year and there was a company there selling exhausts and manifolds. They subsequently made manifolds for us but every time we had a dispatch of kits

Below: Current 2B project has been a big hit. Round tube chassis a significant feature of this car, along with archaic sliding pillar front suspension.

they could never produce enough.

"We decided we'd make our own and we bought a tube bending machine. The manufacturer recommended a specific model and it was absolutely magic. The problem was it would make these manifold tubes in just half an hour and it meant the machine was standing idle for the rest of the month, so that's when we got the idea of making a tubular chassis."

The Robin Hood 2B was launched, featuring not only a large 38mm tubular chassis, but other typically innovative features such as an 'alligator' hinging bonnet arrangement which included the complete scuttle and dash area. Perhaps most intriguing was the company's return to seemingly archaic, sliding pillar front suspension, previously only championed by Morgan. Using components salvaged from the Sierra's front strut arrangement, it was perhaps the most extraordinary case of lateral thinking that we'd ever come across!

The 2B remains in production and, most recently, Robin Hood has redesigned the front suspension and, as an option, reverted back to a more visually appealing and dynamic double wishbone design. Designed to run alongside the 2B, as the ultimate budget package, is Robin Hood's brand new model, the Sub K.

Typical of the company's distinctive way of doing business are its mass collection days. "There's always been the need to instruct people when they collect kits," explains Richard. "If you can get two people to come at the same time then you can talk to them both. If you can get 100 people to come in one day, that's even better. On the last dispatch we did a hundred kits. We started off at 8 o'clock and everyone was gone and we were at MacDonalds by 4 o'clock – it was all over."

Easing the production and dispatch process is another reason why Robin Hood has always tended to offer comprehensive kits rather than giving customers the option of buying just a body or chassis. "If you're buying competitively for your goods, you

Above right: Double wishbone front suspension is an optional upgrade on the 2B. Most customers now go this route unless they're on a tight budget. Below: Spacious interior a big feature of all Robin Hoods.

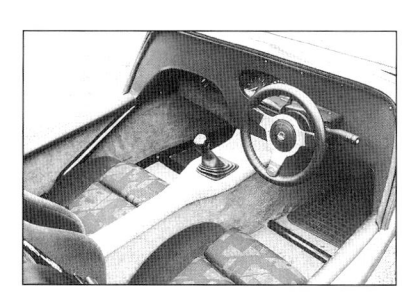

Alligator hinging bonnet a typical novelty of the 2B and most recent Sub K.

can pass the benefit onto your customers. If you pitch your product at a price people can afford, then there's no reason why they shouldn't have it all in one go."

But that's been a policy which has proved more difficult to impose on the company's sideline business,

83

Above: Sub K launched at the 2002 Stafford kit car show. Big feature of this new car, apart from the price, is its micro-strut front suspension arrangement.

Lolocost. "More recently people have come along and said they're thinking of building a Locost and we can see that this is what we're competing against. Initially we were competing against only the book, but now there are a lot of people out there selling packages to support it. If you can't beat them, then you've got to join them and that's what we've done. We are trying to bulk packages together at Lolocost. For instance, if you buy a chassis you get a free propshaft; if you spend £500 you get a 5% discount; if you spend £1000 you get a 10% discount – so it's in their interest to buy packages from us."

But how low does Richard think prices can realistically go? "It depends whether we're hell bent on retaining this market share that we've got now. At £995 we are making a profit and we're happy to make a relatively small profit – I'm not a man who needs a lot more material things."

With the launch of the new Sub K, it looks as though Robin Hood Engineering is still a force to be reckoned with. Indeed, the company's innovative manufacturing techniques and keen pricing will continue to ensure it remains in the headlines, representing a thorn in the side of its competitors and a welcome retreat for those looking for a bargain.

The factory car

At the time of going to press, the newly launched Sub K wasn't available to drive but the existing 2B remains available as the company's more upmarket model. In standard form, both models are supplied with Robin Hood's most

Left: Sub K looks identical to the 2B but closer inspection reveals the differences. Below: Standard 2-litre injection Sierra engine fits with ease.

Typically comprehensive kit package on display for the launch of the Sub K.

recent 'cornerless' round tube chassis. Onto this must be fixed bodywork which is predominantly of mild steel (except for the nose cone, front wings and rear outer wing sections, which are in fibreglass).

Both Sub K and 2B can then be upgraded (for £200 + VAT) to a mirror-finish stainless steel body package with coloured gelcoat fibreglass panels. Beyond this popular option is what Robin Hood calls its Enhancement Pack (£800 + VAT) including alloys wheels, Recaro seats, stainless 4-branch exhaust manifold and silencer, Sabelt seat harness, bespoke rear coil-over dampers and other simple upgrades. These are all items which can be sourced from the donor car but, for obvious reasons, these upgrades remain a popular option.

So where exactly do the Sub K and 2B vary? In overall layout and dimensions they are essentially very similar, but there are significant differences when you dig a little deeper. Most obviously, the 2B uses a sliding pillar front suspension set-up which can be upgraded to a more conventional double wishbone affair if desired by the builder. On the Sub K you're limited to a micro strut front suspension arrangement. Under the skin there is also no upgrade for the Sub K from a mild steel chassis to the stainless chassis option available on the 2B, while the latter kit also has a generally higher specification package for your £1295 + VAT base price.

At £995 + VAT, the Sub K is a seriously competitive kit package which Robin Hood claims will supply everything needed to get a base car on the road – except for one Sierra donor car. The Sub K in the pictures could theoretically be assembled for just £1348, Robin hood allowing £995 for the kit, a budget boot rack at £25, VAT on these at £178, £30 for paint, £20 for odd sundries and £100 for the donor Sierra. While that's obviously a stripped-to-the-bone guide price, it would probably be fair to say that you could realistically get a Sub K roadworthy for under £2000, and that still represents astonishing value.

As for the 2B, as Robin Hood's upmarket model it isn't what you might call expensive. As you'll see from the owner's experience in the next section, including the upgrade packages he managed to get his car on the road for under £3500, and without these upgrades it seems quite feasible to trim £1000 off that price.

So what's a 2B like? When we drove the company's original prototype we were hugely impressed by the package but had reservations about the sliding pillar front suspension package. While the set-up worked fine on smoother A-roads it wasn't so accomplished on rougher back lanes, where we felt the limited suspension travel became a drawback, affecting not only the ride but also the car's braking efficiency. It's almost certainly one reason why Robin Hood offers its upgrade package of a double wishbone front set-up and, at just £150 + VAT, we doubt many customers stick with the standard arrangement.

Hop into the 2B and you're immediately aware of one of the company's big selling points – there's bucket-loads of space. The original Sierra seats are soft and comfy and the complete interior is extremely user friendly – all of which is hardly surprising considering the comprehensive use of the donor components. The Sierra's original dashpod works well enough and Robin Hood has even found room under

Last Robin Hood we drove was this 2B demo car which worked fine, although we weren't convinced by the sliding pillar front suspension. Seemed to work better on customer's car overleaf.

the scuttle to fit the donor's heating system.

Initial driving impression is one of solidity. The 2B isn't as small as some of its competitors, but there's no real hint of scuttle shake or other nasties. There also appears to be very little roll from the front end, although at slower speeds the steering feels pretty heavy and sluggish.

But on-the-limit handling and performance have never been major deciding factors in the purchase of previous Robin Hood models, and we doubt they'll affect the decisions of future 2B or Sub K customers. Of far more importance will be the simplicity of the build, the thoroughly comprehensive nature of the Robin Hood kit package and, of course, the price. The Sub K's potentially sub £2000 completion budget will take some beating.

The customer car

Since the latest Sub K has only just come on the market, it's impossible for us to find a builder who can verify how the build process has gone and how much he's ended up spending. As such, we've looked at an existing 2B project.

Reg Bridgman is a retired aircraft engineer and his wife Ann expressed concerns with his existing hobby. "I used to have an 18ft boat in the drive and my wife and son said they didn't like me going out in the boat and why didn't I build a kit car?" With son Andrew in the midst of a Tiger Cat build (see Chapter 6), it didn't seem such a bad idea, and the trio headed off to their nearest kit car show in Exeter to see what was about.

"I based my budget," remembers Reg, "on the fact that I could sell my boat for about £4000." It meant his options were reasonably limited, and while he'd considered a three-wheeler, Ann was immediately struck by the shining stainless bodywork of Robin Hood's 2B demo car. Building a Tiger Cat like his son Andrew might have been an obvious choice but Reg found he simply

Above: Plenty of room in owner's 2B. Seats came within the standard factory upgrade pack.

couldn't get comfortable in the Cat's comparatively tight cockpit – something that wasn't a problem in the 2B.

Having spent the day at the show, Reg was so confident in his choice that he put down a deposit there and then. Ordering both the company's stainless package and Enhancement Pack meant the shiny stainless panelling, Recaro seats, alloys and a number of other goodies left off the more basic kit. At £2385 it was already a substantial chunk of his budget, but he wouldn't require a great deal more beyond sourcing his own donor car.

When a collection day was announced, Reg and Andrew hired a truck and went up to Robin Hood's Nottingham base along with seemingly hundreds of other customers. "There were so many people there that it was very difficult to get in and out," remembers Reg. "Very cleverly, Richard has got all the parts on a big trolley and you stand at your trailer and hand each other the bits and check them off against a list. Some of the parts are a bit

Reg Bridgman has every reason to look pleased, having made an excellent job of his 2B. Below: Sliding pillar front suspension seems to work well on his car.

difficult to recognise and we were missing some bits. But they went back into the stores and found them."

Having already stripped down an old Sierra donor car, Reg was fully prepared for the build and his aircraft engineering skills certainly gave him confidence when it came to fitting the stainless steel panelling. Stainless is notoriously tricky to work with when it comes to cutting, drilling or bending – and drilling is a key part of fixing the pre-cut panels to the tubular chassis. "To drill stainless steel you need a lot of drill bits. It's so easy to snap them off," explains Reg. "You put a bit of masking tape over the hole you're going to drill and mark the spot, and that helps to keep it in the right place."

While a lot of Robin Hood owners tend to modify their cars, Reg was determined to keep his to exactly standard specification, even to the point of ordering the same red fibreglass body panels that he and Ann had seen on the factory demonstrator. "I spent on average about three hours on the car every day for a year.

"I looked at the build video the night before and the build was pretty straightforward other than installing the steering assembly where it passed the 4-branch exhaust." The latter was one of the few optional extras Reg had ordered from Robin Hood (instead of the standard two-branch manifold that came with the kit), and he found the steering column passed extremely close to the manifold.

Other than the build videos supplied with the kit, there were no other notes or build information other than the company's technical help line. Manned by Robin Hood's main man, Richard Stewart, the service Reg received whenever he phoned up with a query impressed him greatly.

Having spent £400 having the 1600cc Pinto engine refurbished by a local company, one might have expected Reg's seemingly tight budget to come under pressure. However, it's a testament to the comprehensive nature of the Robin Hood package that, including buying the donor and having the engine work done, Reg only spent an additional £900 over the cost of the kit. As such, his car hit the road for just under £3500 – a terrific achievement when you look around the car

While Robin Hood recommended taking the car for its SVA test before fitment of the windscreen (and therefore not having to have a heater and demisting facility), Reg was determined that the car should pass in its fully-finished form. All was going well at the Taunton SVA test centre until the inspector came across slight problems with both the handbrake and front seat location points which, in standard form, allowed the stainless panels to pant (flex) when put under load. Sadly, this wasn't something that Reg could rectify on site, so a second test was booked a couple of weeks later and the problems easily solved back at home with some additional bracing.

Having done some 2500 miles since its completion, the Robin Hood 2B is running smoothly and is completely sorted. The 1600cc engine means this isn't a fire-breathing monster, but it suits its owner's needs perfectly. Reg's car also features the sliding pillar front suspension set-up and through the twisting back lanes of his local Cornish roads the car performs admirably and without any unusual traits. Inside, there's plenty of room while the production car Recaro seats are comfortable and supportive.

Reg has done a superb job with his Robin Hood and the end result works well and delivers everything that he had hoped for. It may not be a back road screamer like Andrew's Tiger Cat but Reg never had it in mind to create anything other than an open top roadster for summer fun. In that respect the Robin Hood has proved perfect. Plus, of course, it hasn't stretched the bank balance unduly.

Chapter Eleven

Jas Buggy

The company

JAS Speedkits may be a relatively new name to the kit car industry, but the company's founder is no stranger to the world of wacky component cars. "It goes back to '69," recalls John Davies, "when I bought a beach buggy from GP." But he didn't just buy a kit; instead he ended up working for GP's John Jobber shortening VW floorpans and assembling fully built cars for those who couldn't be bothered to do the spannering themselves.

It was John Jobber and his GP operation that first brought the beach buggy craze to the UK one year earlier, in 1968. Based on a South African buggy kit called the Lolette, the GP Buggy was an instant hit and at its height GP was taking orders at a rate of 100 per month! John Davies remained employed by GP for the next three years before going self-employed but remaining as GP's primary car builder and chassis technician – and that's how it remained up until around 1998!

Over the years John has built just about every type

Above: JAS Buggies' John Davies worked with buggy icon John Jobber for many years building, amongst other things, the slightly strange GP Madison.

Faithful to the original concept, the JAS Buggy looks absolutely superb and, significantly, is cheap to build.

of kit car launched by the prolific GP operation, from the original Buggy to the 'supercar' styled Centron, ostentatious Madison and, latterly, the evergreen GP Spyder. Meanwhile, he's also managed to maintain his other interest – motorsport. "I've always been involved with the racing side of it and that's what my passion is. It was oval racing and stock cars back in the Sixties. While I was involved with the beach buggies in the Seventies, we did autocross with them (and Centrons) and then from the mid-Seventies we went into off-road racing with the All-Wheel-Drive Club." More recently, it's been a return to the stock car scene but the involvement with GP has gone on throughout.

While GP had sold on the Buggy project some ten year ago, it wasn't until John Jobber decided to sell the GP Spyder in 1998 that John Davies took the decision to set out on his own. His recent marriage to Sharon had provided the catalyst for the new project that was already in the planning stages and which now

Simple fibreglass body tub is dropped over a shortened VW Beetle floorpan.

took centre stage.

"I used to be absolutely buggy mad," explains Sharon. "I always wanted a buggy when I was a teenager but I never got one. So I kept asking him to do one and it took me eighteen months to finally persuade him." Even then John wasn't convinced. "I didn't really think it was going to be a success to be honest," he says. "I thought we'd sell one or two but it was Sharon that pushed me into it – and fortunate that she did!"

Over the years there have been a myriad of different buggy designs. GP was directly responsible for no less than four while the company's original Buggy spawned endless rip-offs alongside other original designs that all came and went during the Seventies. But for John the decision as to a style for his own buggy was easy. "John set about designing the plug," remembers Sharon, "and he wanted to get it back to an original look, but with a few little modifications."

The original GP Buggy was extremely short, offering minimal legroom for the driver and certainly no chance of any rear seat passengers. Both were problems that John wanted to address, without simply reverting to an unmodified Beetle floorpan. Hacking out 12" from the Beetle instead of 15" as in the original GP Buggy, he managed to retain that quintessentially 'short' look while accommodating taller drivers along with young children in the back.

As for the look of the new car, John's always been a fan of the original stripped back buggy style, so the windscreen remains a basic aluminium affair and there are no

Above: It was John's wife Sharon who persuaded him to do the buggy, Sharon having been a lifelong buggy enthusiast.

side panels in the standard JAS Buggy kit (although they will be offered as an option). Having begun preparation of the mould in August of '98, the first road-going car hit the road just five months later in January 1999. The JAS Buggy had arrived and the serious business of selling kits to the public could begin.

89

Over the last three years John And Sharon (hence JAS) have pushed the product hard with a concerted advertising campaign and reasonably regular show appearances. As possibly the only buggy manufacturer in the UK whose only income is generated through the kits, getting the packaging right and running the operation in a professional manner has been critical. JAS prides itself in being able to offer not just the basic kit package but every last nut and bolt needed to assemble a car up to completion. Along with the inevitable full builds, the company has been encouragingly busy and, while sales are never likely to reach 100 a month, interest in the buggy is once again gaining momentum.

JAS currently operates from a small workshop beside John's house, and with the bodywork moulded by outside specialists and no chassis fabrication to worry about, there's plenty of room. So this isn't a fancy industrial unit and you won't find loads of staff dashing

JAS Buggy doesn't pretend to be anything other than a fun car and, in that respect, it's unbeatable.

Above left: Ultra simple interior in keeping with buggy ethos. Above: Rear seats at least mean the kids can enjoy the fun too!

about making bits and dealing with queues of customers. This is a personal little operation where you're guaranteed John and Sharon's undivided attention and also their unflinching enthusiasm for the product.

The factory car

JAS's first demonstrator was pink, a colour chosen, not surprisingly, by Sharon and it worked remarkably well. She's also scanned the 502 different colour options available and come up with the light blue used with the current car – like the pink, it works a treat. From the first time you see the JAS you can see that John has completely succeeded in his self-imposed design brief – this is unquestionably a beach buggy in the traditional sense with no frills or funny design quirks to deflect your attention away from the basic design. The proportions look great, the lack of side panels accentuates the car's aggressive low front and kicked-up rear. This is a beach buggy, pure and simple.

Fit and finish on this demo car are spot on, although there's not a great deal to complicate matters. Inside, the car has the luxury of a carpet set while the Cobra bucket seats and JAS rear bench look just perfect. Overall, the aluminium windscreen frame, stainless steel roll-over bar (largely cosmetic) and front and rear nudge bars give off just the right amount of flash, while the gleaming engine and its ancillaries form a glinting jewel to be ogled at by passers by.

Even a cursory glance around the JAS is enough to bring a smile to your face. This is such a fun looking car. There are no illusions of grandeur, this isn't a sports car, it isn't a practical car, it's not a fancy car and it's certainly not a serious car – it's just a fun car. You know you're in for a giggle before you've even fired up the Beetle engine.

Hop in and the bucket seat is easily adjusted on its runners and a reasonable driving position is quickly found. The Beetle's floor mounted pedals always take a little getting used to, especially the long floor-hinging accelerator. Ahead of you is an ultra simple dash with, in this case, just one speedo gauge while through the large windscreen the flared wings kick out on either side of you. From here it's easy to see how the bodywork is dropped down onto the Beetle's platform chassis, since all the bolts are still clearly visible in the interior. This aptly demonstrates just how straightforward the assembly ought to be.

Fire up the 1641cc lump used in this car and the cannon exhausts do just as their name suggests – this car sounds fantastic! The gear change is encouragingly smooth and we're quickly off and away. For all its aural promise, the Beetle engine is never likely to be a barn-stormer, but it's hardly relevant and the JAS is nevertheless brisk.

Despite the bodyshell's bonded-in tub, there is no further strengthening structure above the basic Beetle floorpan, and that's immediately apparent with a degree of scuttleshake coming through the steering wheel. Indeed, hit potholes and poorer road surfaces and the limited torsional rigidity of the set-up is apparent. Some form of metal triangulated subframe

Latest cars have this new windscreen surround which is not only neater, but also stronger.

Above: Lack of side panels gives the JAS Buggy a classical look.

to the bodywork would work wonders here and, with the addition of full side panels, need not be overly visible.

It's a feature JAS is aware of and one we suspect will be addressed in the near future. However, it should be stressed that at no time does the JAS feel unsafe and its performance always remains utterly acceptable. Brakes will be another feature of any beach buggy that will often trade at the acceptable level of performance rather than the peak. Most donors will come with drums at each corner. However, the current demo car does feature disc brakes as a result of its late year donor, and retro fitting front discs need not be a major problem, especially on the basis that the donor's suspension is likely to need comprehensive refurbishing anyway.

Blasting about in the JAS demonstrator, it's simply impossible not to have fun. From the styling to the sound and the outrageous effect the car has on anyone who sees it, the JAS is a complete hoot and, thankfully, falls well within our self-imposed price bracket. Talking through the figures with John and Sharon it's clear that a cleanly built example should hit the road from about £3800 including a full set of weather gear, decent wheels and tyres and a proper engine dress-up kit (although leaving the builder to shorten the chassis). To have a car as cool as this, that's got to be a bargain.

The customer car

Jim Brown has spent much of his life building model aeroplanes and the single garage beside his house could be more accurately described as a hangar, such is the number of remote controlled models stored there. So one thing was for sure – if he was to build a car it wouldn't be happening in the garage!

While Jim's always maintained his own cars, he's never got round to building one, although he did nearly buy a beach buggy many years ago. "I've always liked beach buggies," he comments. "When I was a kid I went to buy one and the bloke wanted £100 for it. I offered him £75 and he said yes, but when I went back to get it he had already sold it for £100 to someone else."

While he never pursued the specialist car interest further at the time, more recently a mate of his got him thinking about hot rods. "I was looking for a Ford Pop with a Rover V8 in it," remembers Jim, "and we found one for sale in *Which Kit?* but it was already sold. I saw an advert for a beach buggy and I thought it looked absolutely cracking." The ad in question belonged to JAS Speedkits and the pared back, original buggy styling of the JAS demonstrator really brought back the memories.

Jim's initial thought was to buy a second-hand one via the magazine's classifieds, but rather than having a car which has been built by someone else he soon realised that in order to get a car in the colour and with the finishing details that he wanted he would have to build it himself. He first got details from a number of current buggy manufacturers, but he felt most confident dealing with John and Sharon at JAS. "John said you could build one for about £3000," Jim remembers, "so I thought I'd work on about £4000 so that I could have exactly what I wanted."

With only limited space in front of the garage, Jim built himself a car port under which he could assemble the car. With space enough for just one car, he decided he had to strip down the donor Beetle and prepare it

You won't find a more enthusiastic kit car owner than Jim Brown – his overwhelming passion for the car is infectious.

to a state at which the new buggy shell could be put in place as soon as it arrived. As such, the first job was to find a suitable donor. Jim freely admits that he really didn't know what he was looking for, except that it had to have a beam axle front suspension set-up rather than later MacPherson struts. He also realised that if he found an early car he may also be able to keep the buggy as tax exempt.

Initial research threw up some high priced cars but his local paper eventually produced a likely contender, up for grabs for just £250. As it turned out, the 1600cc engine was a reconditioned unit and several of the bits he needed had been recently serviced. Not that it looked that way when he got the car back home. His wife, Shirley, couldn't quite believe the state of what she saw in front of her and even Jim was a little taken aback by the Beetle's vague steering and generally shabby condition – it was one of those moments when you wonder whether the whole thing has been a complete waste of time.

Stripping down really ancient donor cars can often be a real pain because nothing simply unbolts and everything has rusted solid. But because Jim was only really after the suspension and the central spine section of the Beetle's floorpan he found the strip down easy – anything that wouldn't budge was simply cut off and discarded. With the rotten floorpan sections cut off, there didn't seem to be very much left of the original donor, and Jim took what remained right back to bare metal, including all the suspension parts.

The JAS buggy requires the floorpan to be shortened and Jim didn't fancy doing that himself, so he called on the expertise of his hot rod friend, who was something

With 502 different gelcoat colours to choose from, Jim eventually went for red!

of a dab-hand when it came to welding. Following the clear instructions given by JAS, all the necessary cuts were made, the shortened sections all lined up and the floorpan welded back together (along with brand new floor sections).

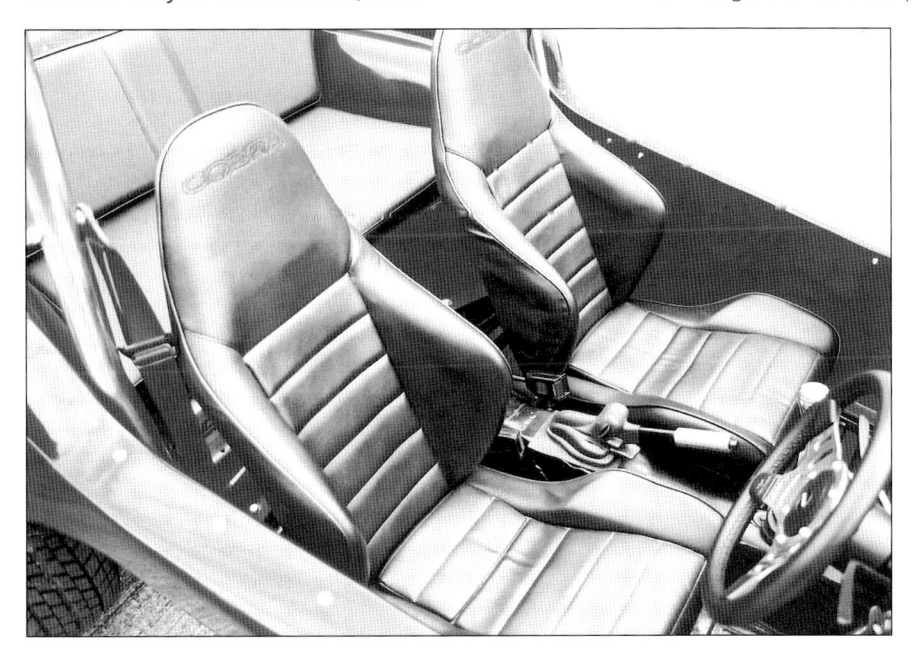

With the suspension fully reconditioned and painted with black Smoothrite, the reassembled floorpan really began to look the part. Now was the time to order the bodyshell. When Jim phoned up JAS to find out about his colour options, he expected John Davies to give him perhaps a dozen different colours to choose from, but when he was told there were over 502 different gelcoat colours he had to do a bit more thinking. Not that it made much difference – he still ended up with red!

Jim had begun stripping down the Beetle in August 2001, with the idea being to finish the car in time for the next summer, but he was already ordering the bodyshell just a month later and the car would actually hit the streets by November of the same year – this was not a complicated build. Having collected the bright

Cobra Roadster 7 seats work well in the simple interior. They're comfortable, too.

Using almost exclusively brand new parts, Jim's Buggy has cost around £4500 so it should be possible to trim quite a bit off that if you're on a tighter budget.

red shell from JAS, his rolling chassis was soon transformed. "Within two hours," remembers Jim, "you were looking at something that resembled a buggy."

The rest of the build moved along equally swiftly, Jim sticking to largely standard JAS specification but going his own way with Cobra Roadster 7 seats. Other touches include the retention of the Beetle speedo which required some subtle mods in order to make it fit in perfectly. The rear view mirror is another lovely feature, a pass-on from the custom car scene.

Jim reckons the final bill for his buggy is about £4500 but for that he says he's got an almost brand new car. When it comes to value for money he's in little doubt. "It's something that I am so proud of. For smiles per miles it is brilliant – you just can't beat it. To me it is the best £4500 I have ever spent." And Jim is certainly pleased with his latest toy. Walk past his house and the chances are you'll be invited for a ride – his neighbours, their children and most people along his road have already been out in the car. Here's a man who's unquestionably reliving his youth – and loving every minute of it!

A quick run out in the car with him certainly confirms that the beach buggy remains a real blast – it's a giggle a minute and everyone who sees you gives a big smile. There's nothing pretentious about a buggy. It's just made for fun, as simple as that. What's more, Jim has made an amazing job of assembling his car – everything looks meticulously built and the engine, gearbox and suspension all appear in tip-top condition. In terms of value for money, there seems little doubt that the JAS could be assembled for less than his £4500 outlay but, as Jim points out, his car is virtually brand new. So is it good value for money? Absolutely fantastic – we loved it.

Chapter Twelve

Locost

The book

So far we've dealt with what one might call traditional kit cars – cars supplied by a manufacturer in a kit form usually consisting of at least a chassis and body package. The Locost does not fall into this category since, in its most original format, the car is completely assembled by the private enthusiast using guidance from a book – no pre-formed chassis, coloured gelcoat fibreglass bodywork or anything else.

From our perspective it means that you're not paying for anyone else's labour, and that, dear friends, means it is possible to build a Locost very, very cheaply. While rumour has it that one car has hit the road for under fifty pounds, many enthusiasts have completed cars for sub £1000 while the average Locost build now rests at about £1500. So while the effort required to assemble a Locost may be greater than with a conventional kit car, the pay-off in terms of reduced outlay is obvious.

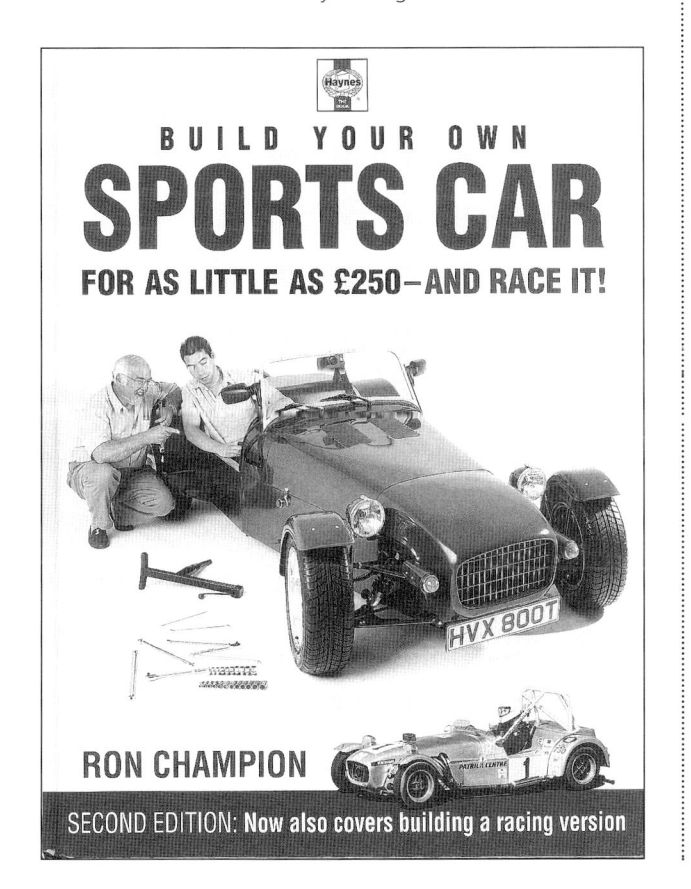

Ron Champion, the man behind the hugely successful book, Build Your Own Sports Car For As Little As £250.

As such, it's not surprising to learn that the book responsible for all this activity has sold over 100,000 copies world-wide and is still going strong. Launched in 1996, *Build Your Own Sports Car For As Little As £250* was written by Ron Champion who was, at the time, head of Design and Technology at Oundle School, in Northampton.

Ten years earlier Ron had joined the private school to give instruction in Motor Engineering to the school's CCF (Combined Cadet Force) "I was in charge of the REME section (Royal Electrical and Mechanical Engineering)," recalls Ron. "We used to strip down Land Rovers that were donated by the army and on one occasion we had a Ferret scout car which was great fun.

"Historically the school had always had an involvement with motor engineering. At the turn of the century it had a very forward-looking headmaster and he had the second motor vehicle in Oundle. His coachman had been with the manufacturer of the car for a month learning to be a driver and mechanic, and every time the car needed attention the headmaster got all the boys assembled in the Blacksmith's shop to watch what was going on."

Realising the potential impact of cars on everyday

Above: Peter and James Mann were two enthusiasts to complete their cars quickly, including making their own distinctive fibreglass wings and bonnets. Above right: Steve Mullany's example was another to catch the eye of Which Kit? *magazine.*

life, the headmaster was keen to show the boys how the car worked and since then the school's pro-active tuition has yielded impressive results. "Over the years there were a number of significant boys at Oundle," comments Ron. "One called Morgan, another called Raymond Mays (of ERA and BRM etc) as well as Herbert Austin."

When Ron's son, James, was getting close to driving age the subject of a first car was an inevitable question. "He had his mind set on a kit car but as a humble school teacher there was no way I could afford one, so I said I would make him one. So we built the first car and I finished it off at the school because they had facilities for spraying. All the kids saw it and asked what it was. I said it was nothing really but that it was meant to look like a Lotus Seven."

Keen to get in on the act, the students asked whether it would be possible to build one at the school, and within a month two more chassis had been produced and three cars completed within the first year. "The most wonderful thing about working with young people," observes Ron, "is that their problem solving starts with a clean sheet of paper, unlike adults who resort to previous experience.

"I realised during my time as a teacher that experience is a handicap because it doesn't make you think. If you don't have experience you sit down and solve a problem and sometimes the problems are solved in really unique ways. Very occasionally I would set pupils tasks and they would come back with a solution which I realised would work – I would think why didn't I think of that? So it was incredibly exciting and rewarding and I got a big kick out of it."

But it wasn't only the kids who were impressed with Ron's creations. Staff members quickly began suggesting that Ron should write a book about building the car. Having collected a large number of drawings and pictures of the three cars as they were assembled, Ron wrote a few draft chapters and sent them off to Haynes Publishing and asked whether or not the publisher would be interested. Almost by return of post, a contract was in the bag.

"In the 1950s and 60s there were several books on building your own car (one of them by John Haynes himself) so if you wanted to try your hand you could find a book. You couldn't in the Nineties and I realised there was a gap in the market. As I started writing it I

Ron poses for a promotional shot for his book, while son James takes it easy in the cockpit.

became more and more excited, and I've got to admit that it became a race against time because I thought it was so obvious that if I didn't get this book done, someone else was going to beat me to it."

Actually sitting down and writing a lengthy book was not something Ron Champion had ever done before and it wasn't something he particularly enjoyed. Having always been a hands-on man, tapping away on a keyboard was a discipline he was ill-prepared for, but the book was eventually completed and Haynes set about the promotion bandwagon with a vengeance...

"The reaction from the mainstream media was fantastic – all the papers ran a story and I was also on eight or nine TV shows with the car." But if the response was unanimously positive from the mainstream press, there were less than enthusiastic words from the kit car magazines. "From the specialist market the reaction was terrible," remembers Ron. "Most people thought it could never be done and you couldn't get people to weld up chassis because it was a specialist skill.

"Well, when I wrote the book I knew that back in the Fifties and Sixties you did have people doing it and things haven't changed that much. So I got a bit of a spanking from the specialist market which was very upsetting for me as a person. I was extremely disappointed. But over the next year the book sales just went and went and went. To my knowledge none of the cars has ever failed due to bad workmanship."

If the specialist press had been hesitant, the enthusiastic public was lapping it up, and it was soon very clear that those who previously had never considered a kit car because of the expense had now found an outlet for their automotive hobby. Not only that, but the car was also attracting a following from those who were positively attracted to the idea of building something from scratch rather than simply purchasing parts from a conventional kit car supplier.

While Ron may be a hands on man, he's not half bad at promotion and, with the might of Haynes to back him up, the Locost phenomenon was soon a real force to be reckoned with, with hugely successful world-wide sales and a one-make race series quickly established within the UK.

Not surprisingly, following the success of the book a number of fabricators began to offer the parts that builders were struggling to make or source

Locost Car Club has gone from strength to strength.

themselves. Before long you could not only buy wishbones but complete chassis assemblies from a variety of sources, so that if you weren't confident with a welder you could still go ahead with the project, albeit at slightly greater cost.

Realising the scale of the success he had on his hands, Ron Champion finally decided to concentrate full time on the Locost and stepped down from his teaching position at Oundle. With others now offering a wide variety of parts based around his book, Ron himself got in on the act by lending his backing to the formation of Locost Limited. Offering absolutely everything from a wishbone to a complete car, the venture hasn't been as successful as the book itself and, at the time of writing, the company's future is in question.

It didn't take long for various companies to start offering pre-fabricated chassis and body components. Stuart Taylor Motorsport (below) was one of the first.

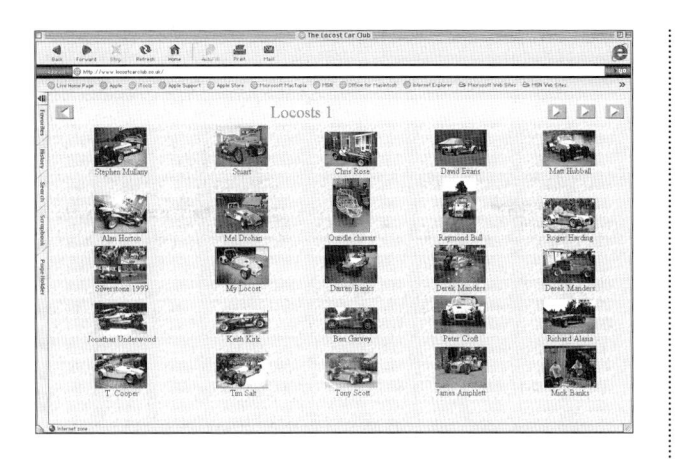

Above: Locost Car Club website is hugely popular and is always stuffed full of regularly updated material.

Indeed, Ron is the first to admit that not all of his business activities have been as successful as the book and, fundamentally, he remains an enthusiast. With a second edition of the book updated to include information on Single Vehicle Approval and preparation of a car for competition use, the Locost phenomenon still has a full head of steam. "You can see cars in Malaysia, Australia, New Zealand, Thailand, India, all over America, Canada, South America, the Greek Islands," comments Ron. "At the moment I'm in Spain and I've just had a Locost homologated over there. I think it is the first Spanish-built sports car to be homologated and I've had a lot of coverage with the Spanish press. I've also had approval from the Spanish race car association to run a one-make race series. So it's all systems go."

And he's not kidding. Haynes has also just launched Ron's latest book, *Build Your Own Buggy For £100*. If Ron wasn't sure of what to expect with the first book, he certainly has high hopes for this latest venture with, typically, a number of innovative promotional tricks up his sleeve. Judging from the success of *Build Your Own Sports Car For As Little As £250* you'd be a brave man to bet against him.

"I see myself as an enthusiast," says Ron. "Someone once described me as the Fred Dibnah of the kit car industry and I quite like that."

The club

With no official manufacturer to back-up enthusiasts, a highly pro-active club was always going to be critical, but despite attempts to start something a year after the book's launch it wasn't until 1998 that the Locost Car Club was officially formed. However, since that shaky start the club, like the book itself, hasn't looked back.

"We started with 300 members in the first year," recalls club secretary Rory Perrett. "It increased to 500 in the second and now we're up to about 800. Initially, there weren't many cars on the road and there weren't any suppliers. The club was all about providing information and technical support. Where to find bits and that sort of thing."

Today the club is well established, with over 140 completed cars on the books, a quarterly newsletter and highly active website. "It seems to be quite an internet based thing," comments Rory. "People who build cars seem to be into the internet as well. In addition to the club website there's also an extremely active mailbase, which is an international one on Yahoo with well over 1000 members."

Support for those building cars is still the club's core responsibility, with those asking for advice being put in touch with existing members who are also building a similar specification car. While the original Locost is a Ford Escort-based machine, builders have now used a variety of different donors and, of course, engine options are hugely varied.

With so many companies now offering chassis and body packs for the Locost, are the majority of owners now shunning away from welding their own chassis? Steve Gibbons, club treasurer, thinks not. "They're buying a lot more of the parts that are available now but the majority are still building their chassis. There

Club secretary Rory Perrett has been building his car for several years, putting aside £5 per week and aiming for a car on the road for around £750!

Jim Luke (foreground) and Keith Kirk (standing) built their cars together, with each hitting the road for under £2000.

are two types of people with the Locost – those who can only afford to build one and those who want to build a car from scratch."

But the availability of pre-fabricated components is certainly having an effect on the average Locost build. "The first cars that were on the road were between £750 – £1200," comments Rory. "Now I would say the average is £2500. It is still possible to build a car for under £1000 but it seems that people no longer wish to, and they are quite happy to spend the extra money to get the adjustable shock absorbers, trim etc."

Not that Rory has been swayed by the onset of aftermarket goodies in relation to the assembly of his own Locost. "I'd always wanted a kit car but I couldn't bring myself to write a cheque for £2500 in one go. So I said I'd put aside a fiver a week." Five years later, he's currently in credit and hoping for a complete car on the road for less than £700!

Of course, as more cars hit the road so the demands on the club change. "It's now more about booking up track days and shows – the traditional club things," observes Rory. "The membership has also stabilised. We get quite a high turnover because people buy the book, get enthusiastic, join the club and never start. We also get people who join the club and build the car, but they're not clubby people so they then drop out."

At the centre of all this remains Ron Champion's book, *Build Your Own Sports Car For As Little As £250*, and while most builders appreciate that they'll be spending more than £250, the book gives them the confidence to get started. "The book gets vaguer and vaguer the further into it you go. The chassis is almost like an A-Z – fit Part A to Part B. Everybody looks at the chassis chapter and follows it religiously, but by the time they get to the fitting out they pick the book up once a month."

With such good guidance for the assembly of the chassis, the most frequently asked questions by those who've started usually centre around the suspension wishbones, sourcing suitable coil-over dampers and finding an aftermarket source for the scuttle section of the car which is notoriously tricky to make.

For those yet to make a start, there's always the worry about welding up a chassis from a pile of metal tubes. But neither Rory or Steve feels it needs to be a stumbling block. If you can cut up the tubing and tack weld it together then the chances are that you can find someone who is proficient with a welder to do the serious welding for you at minimal cost. Alternatively, even if you have to pay £30 an hour to get a

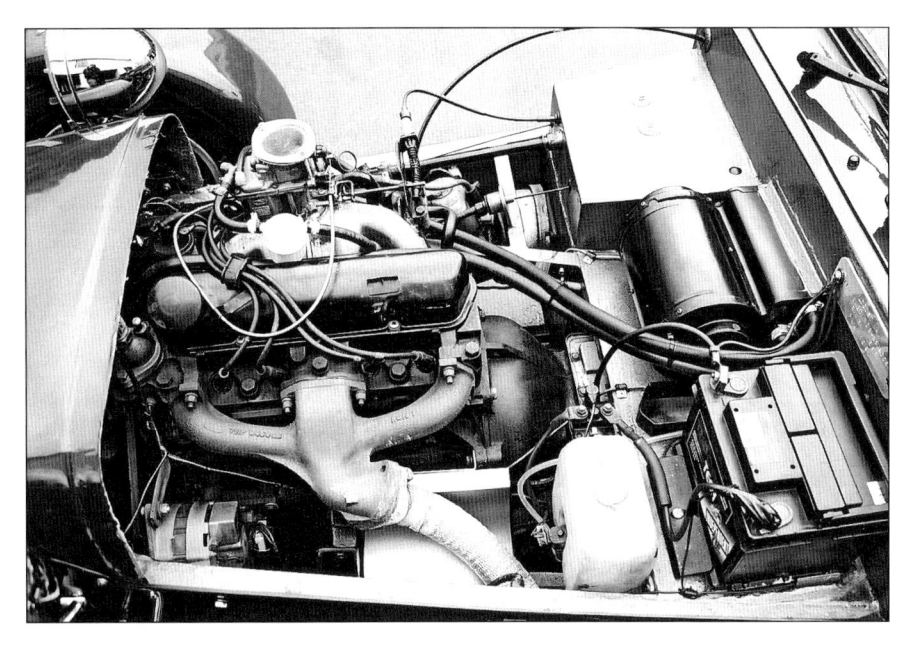

Above and below: Both cars use standard 1300cc X-flow engines. Keith's car (above) has the slightly tidier engine bay while also seeing regular action.

professional to finish off the job, it'll only be a morning's work – so still considerably cheaper than buying a pre-assembled chassis.

And despite lots of people telling us that it's easy to learn how to weld, the important thing to remember is that there's no pressure to do everything yourself. "If you're in doubt," says Rory, "get a professional."

The owners

On the assumption that no two Locosts will look the same, we were surprised to find that Keith Kirk and Jim Luke's cars bear an uncanny similarity. While the colours may be different and the interior trim isn't the same, there's a surprising number of familiar features common to both cars – surprising, that is, until you realise that Keith works for Jim and both built their cars at the same time!

"We had looked at the book," recalls Keith, "and my nephew had a book as well and he came across and asked whether we might help him. We said we would and, since we were making one, we decided to do three." Ironically, it's Keith's nephew who still hasn't finished so someone, somewhere got the rough deal!

Neither Keith nor Jim even vaguely considered the conventional kit car industry, both for reasons of cost and the fact that they wanted to build the car from the chassis upwards. In this latter respect, they had a distinct advantage – Jim owns a machine shop and Keith works in it as a sheet metal worker – making the chassis simply wasn't an issue. Buying the materials at trade also establishes that these are probably the cheapest chassis on the planet – a measly £18.17p per car!

Once the three chassis had been fabricated, the main assembly work for the cars all occurred back at the various homes of the intrepid trio. "The first thing I ever bought was a steering wheel which I found at an auto jumble," remembers Keith. "I hung it on the garage wall and that gave me the inspiration to finish the car."

Three Ford Escort donor cars were dug out of the local classifieds and arrived together at Jim's yard for stripping down. Interestingly, all of the cars had small 1300cc X-flow engines but it's soon clear that ultimate performance simply wasn't a consideration for any of these builders.

Typically, the Locost chassis is panelled in aluminium, with fibreglass mouldings accounting for the four wings and nose cone. But Keith sourced some Zintec

Both cars have this natty lockable storage box in the boot. Not big but better than nothing.

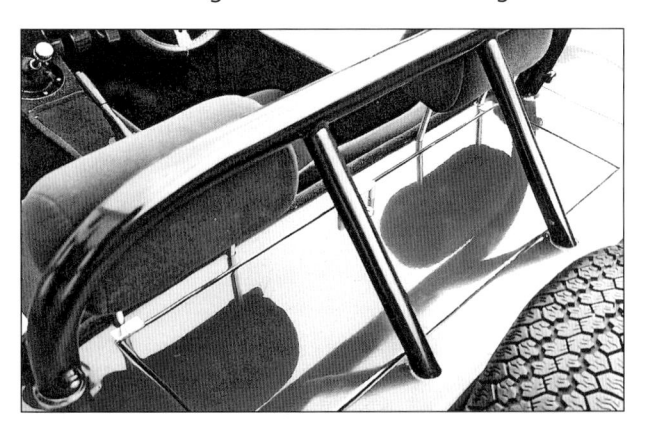

sheets which are a galvanised mild steel. At just £16 each they were considerably cheaper than ally and, since the cars would be painted anyway, the quality of the bare metal finish was immaterial.

Keith's fabrication expertise certainly paid dividends, the trio benefiting from stainless steel Tig-welded wishbones, bespoke pedals and welded roll-over protection. When it came to the tricky choice of coil-over dampers, Keith followed advice from the owners' club and sourced second-hand Reliant Robin items at just £60 a set. Refurbished back at home, they not only look the part but work extremely well, if a little soft on the limit.

Another good deal was struck for the fibreglass panels, a bulk order of three sets trimming the price down to just £100 per car. Once again, because the Locosts would be painted, the panels could be supplied with no gelcoat colour and it was left to the builders to trim the panels to size and prepare them for painting. This is one area where Keith and Jim's cars differ, since Keith decided to blend his rear wings into the bodywork while Jim went for a more conventional look with a plastic bead strip separating the wings from the body tub.

With their inherent fabrication skills, there's little doubt that these two builders progressed at a quick pace, with Jim's car hitting the road first, just 12 months after the chassis was made. Both cars would have to go through Single Vehicle Approval, although their pre-2000 testing allowed them to take advantage of a number of exemptions for which later cars would have to comply (particularly interior and exterior projections). With Jim's car in for its test first, Keith could hopefully put right any problems on his own machine.

As it turned out, problems were few and far between – the most serious being that the seat belt top mounts were too low. Once rectified back in the workshop, Jim's car was quickly on the road. Despite making the necessary modifications to his own car, Keith's Locost also failed at its first attempt – with lower seat mounts being insufficient, some wiring in the engine bay needing additional protection from heat off the exhaust and extra P-clips required for a brake line.

In terms of cost Keith knows precisely how much his car has set him back and, including SVA, the Locost stands him in at just under £1600. While Keith painted his car himself, Jim called in the professionals and an additional £400 for that has lifted his car to nearer £2000 all in.

The result is two of the smartest Locosts we've come across. Jim's car, with its metallic paint and silver stripe is probably the more visually impressive, although the use of Fiesta alloys means the rear wheels are noticeably inset from the arches. On Keith's car it's not such an issue since he's used Mk2 Escort alloys with a more appealing offset.

Top right: Jim's pride and joy is this wood dash. Keith bought his steering wheel before he started the project while his seats were originally in a bank!

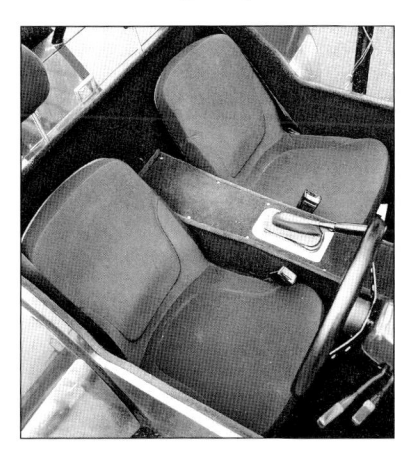

Top and bottom right: Keith has blended-in his fibreglass wings and lights while Jim has kept them all separate. Going your own way is one of the big appeals of a Locost build.

Other exterior features include the unique badging found on both cars. The windscreen pillars on Keith's car show a 'K' emblem while Jim has gone for a more involved 'L7' design ('L' being for Jim's surname and '7' for, well...you know what that stands for!). Bonnet bulges to cover the X-flow air filters also help to identify these cars – Jim's with a slightly incongruous fabricated affair and Keith's being a dainty fibreglass item from Westfield.

In the engine bay of both cars the X-flow lump seems right at home, with good access to all the vital components. A Mini heater deals with SVA requirements for a demisting facility on the windscreen, while a decent pedal box cover keeps the front bulkhead clutter-free.

Inside the cockpit, it's once again each to their own. Jim's pride and joy is the solid walnut dash while Keith's most bizarre purchase was a couple of National Westminster Bank office seats which he modified and had re-trimmed! Perhaps the only things in here which suggest these are budget builds are the donor gauges, but when a full set of aftermarket instruments costs several hundred pounds, these ones begin to make perfect sense.

While a shoulder injury has currently halted Jim's enjoyment of his car, Keith still uses his Locost as often as possible and regardless of the weather (he only has a tonneau cover for it). "You get a lot of enjoyment building them and you get a lot of enjoyment driving them," says Keith, who's currently in the midst of designing a hardtop for his car.

While these builders had a distinct advantage when it came to the fabrication elements of the build, it's also clear from talking to the club that there are affordable alternatives if you're not prepared to do the welding yourself. One thing is for sure, such a stumbling block shouldn't stop you building a Locost, and the sense of achievement from doing everything else on the car will still give you a buzz that few other kit cars can match.

Chapter Thirteen

Paul Banham X21

The company

Paul Banham Conversions has become a major force within the kit car industry in the last few years, pumping out large volumes of affordable kits with pretty and often innovative styling. What makes the company's products quite distinct from other kit cars is the fact that they all retain part or all of the original donor's chassis and running gear, with a simple fibreglass body being dropped over the top.

With no chassis to manufacture (only a few strengthening beams), all of the various models on offer are encouragingly cheap, but it hasn't always been that way. "I started out doing roof conversions in the Seventies," remembers company MD Paul Banham. "The first one was a Morris Minor and then I specialised in British sports cars – MGs, Triumphs and stuff like that." From here things went quickly upmarket. "I bought myself an Aston Martin DBS V8 and chopped the roof off it, and then I continued to do another thirty of them! Along with those, I did DB6s and DB4s."

By the Eighties Banham was firmly established at the upper end of the market, trading in classic cars, undertaking restorations and making a name for himself as a specialist in open-top conversions. "I've had 66 Jensens – the first FF ever made, the Interceptor prototype – I used to do lots of restorations," recalls

The car that's currently Banham's busiest seller is the Metro-based X21.

Paul Banham has been a body conversion specialist for many years although it's only more recently that he's got into the kit car business.

Paul. "Then I did lots of Jaguar conversions – that's probably what I'm more well known for doing. Lots of XJSs and XJ6s into cabriolets, with hard panels and folding back-ends – in Jaguar circles they're very well regarded. That went on into the mid Nineties and I still do woodwork for Jaguars, Range Rovers and Rolls Royces. Much more lucrative than kit cars!"

The progression into kit cars was a gradual one. "We used to build the Jags with wider wings and then obviously cut the roof off. So it was becoming a kit of parts anyway. Then we reshaped it all to make a rounded Jaguar called the SS and then we offered it as a kit in about 1995. That sold a bit but the thing I quickly learned was that the best kit is a small kit."

There were also other factors which encouraged the move away from the classic car scene. "Classic cars fell

103

Left: Big Jaguar conversion was the first Banham product to be sold in kit form. Above: Wood veneer dashboards are still a highly lucrative part of the business.

out of the sky," he recalls. "With things that are very expensive I found that if you go into any sort of economic decline you can get into deep trouble. We had one customer knock us £28,000 – just one customer!" Heading in the opposite direction, Paul found his first kit car donor from an unlikely source. "I'd been playing around with Skodas and I liked the idea of the Skoda because it was strong and very cheap. I was at the Stoneleigh kit car show a good few years ago and Chesil brought a German Porsche 550 replica onto their stand and, over the weekend they had people round it all day and every day. I thought I liked that."

Sourcing a fibreglass 550 replica shell from elsewhere, Paul set about making it fit the Skoda underpinnings. "I stretched it eight inches, four inches in the doors and four inches in the back and put it on the Skoda to create my own 550 kit – I've sold bucket loads of them."

Below: Simple interior suits the Spyder perfectly. There's a huge boot area under the rear deck.

Following the success of the Banham Spyder, Paul was quickly looking for a similarly appealing package and found it in the form of the Banham Sprint, a Frog-eye replica based on a modified Mini. While the Sprint continued the success story, Banham's third creation, a unique 4-seat Skoda-based kit called the Redina, was less well received and the company quickly reverted to the more trusted format of replica manufacture.

Heading bang up to date, Banham came out with the X99 in 1999, an Audi TT inspired body conversion based on the ageing mechanicals of an Austin/Rover Metro. The wild looks and remarkable affordability were an instant hit but he quickly learnt that simplicity was the secret to success. "If you're trying to find someone to make light covers it's a nightmare – we had regular problems with them and it was just too expensive. Normally, the philosophy of a manufacturer is to sell a kit and then sell the customer as much else afterwards. That's not my philosophy. Mine is to stick to the specialised bit, which is the kit, and sell the customer nothing else if you can possibly achieve that."

Below: Porsche replica was the first large volume Banham product. Authentic GRP shell stretched by 8".

Above: Ill-fated Redina one of the few commercial failures for Banham. Right: All was forgiven when the company moved onto the pretty Mini-based Sprint Frogeye replica.

That philosophy was fine-tuned with the back-to-basics SupaBug, an X99 inspired roadster with no doors and conventional front and rear light clusters, but the lack of practicality limited its ultimate appeal. Enter stage left, the X21, Banham's most popular model to date, with conventional doors, a vast boot space and comprehensive weather protection. The company is in no doubt that low prices and dynamite looks are critical to the success of any new project. "We're in a world of declining prices and you've got to join in," states Paul. "When we took our X21 to Stoneleigh for the first time we had people three deep around it for two days and, to me, that's what it takes to have a successful project."

Not that it has all been plain sailing. The stack 'em high, sell 'em cheap philosophy hasn't always endeared the company to the kit car press or other kit car manufacturers. By the very nature of the assembly process, all Banham products require a degree of welding in order to put back the strength that is lost in the donor when its roof is chopped off. That's an anathema to most modern kit car manufacturers and, indeed, many of their customers but, while there's little doubt that some Banham customers fail to complete their projects for all manner of reasons, the appeal of the end product is enough to see most through to completion. "Generally I find the customers are the good guys," says Banham. "As long as you start the kit and you mean to carry on, then you'll finish it. I often say to people to 'just get going on it'."

The factory car

It's easy to see the appeal of Paul Banham's products when you see the X21 for the first time. It's a terrific looking car. With its fancy paint, big MGF-sourced wheels and half-leather interior it looks every bit the modern roadster and absolutely everyone you bump into thinks it's terrific. Credit where credit is due, Paul Banham certainly knows how to press the right buttons, and that's before you tell them the price...

If the dynamite styling draws them in, then the kit price goes for the jugular. At £1795 + VAT for the complete body set and re enforcing metalwork package it sounds pretty encouraging. When you remember that it's based on a cheap-as-chips Metro it sounds even better. Decent paint will lift the price, but we're still talking about a car with modern sports car looks being on the road for well under £5000.

When it comes to the donor car it's always worth remembering that we're talking about everything up to and including the comparatively recent Rover 100 GTi with its terrific K-series 16-valve engine. Find one with light panel damage and prices really tumble – you certainly shouldn't end up paying anything over a grand. As such, we'd suggest it's probably not worth considering older A-series engined cars, which not only offer mundane performance but are also likely to be very rusty. Don't forget that you'll be retaining virtually

First viewing of the Banham X99 at Stoneleigh '99.

Development of the breed. From X99...

...to X99 convertible. Headlight covers sorted for...

all of the donor car, so the better condition it's in, the less repair work you'll have to do.

Then comes the nerve-wracking bit. The front wings un-bolt easily enough, as do the bumpers, doors and tailgate, but then it's time to get a bit brutal with the grinder and cut off the roof, from the bottom of the windscreen pillars to the bottom of the C-pillars at the back. The Metro's windscreen is retained and bonded into the new fibreglass shell that will eventually drop over your revamped Metro.

Stiffening up the Metro is the next job, with vast 100x35mm section 2mm thick tubing being slid down the inside of each sill and welded in place. Because it is going down the inside of the double-skinned Metro sill, it remains completely invisible and doesn't effect the interior space at all (which also means the original carpet set can be retained). Additional A and B-pillar stiffeners are then welded into place while a slightly more complex rear cruciform structure is positioned across the rear of the car behind the rear bench seat (which is moved forward slightly). Paul Banham is the first to admit that this isn't a precision job, merely an exercise in restoring strength to the original Metro monocoque.

With this welding work done (which could always be undertaken by a local garage if you didn't feel up to it yourself), the rest of the assembly is of a more conventional kit car nature. The one-piece main tub is dropped over the Metro and fixed in place by a mixture of riveting and sealing. A metal stiffener around the windscreen surround is welded down onto the new A-posts while the new fibreglass doors bolt onto the original Metro hinge points.

Up front the Metro's bonnet has to be separated from the original frame and the X21 fibreglass bonnet is bonded on in its place. This has the advantage of retaining all the original bonnet hinges and catches.

Current X21 uses repainted Metro interior to great effect. Scorpio leather seats are a good touch.

While there's new flat door glass, the interior door furniture and winding mechanism remain as standard, as does the complete interior. In the green demo car the company has painted the dash and door trims, while the seats are electrically adjustable leather units from a Granada Scorpio.

Outside is where you'll find the few non-donor sourced items which help to give the X21 its upmarket feel. The front headlights are VW Lupo, the rears are after-market Hella items. The door handles are also pinched from VW while the flush-fitting filler cap is an MGF unit. Fitting and lining up the various fibreglass body panels and

...back-to-basics Superbug which naturally led to...

...the current best seller, the Banham X21.

accurately preparing them for paint is going to be critical if you want to end up with a decent finish – and this type of car demands a production car feel to it. Paul Banham estimates building an X21 to the standard of the test car will set you back around £4500-5000, while he's had customers complete the job for as little as £3000.

Under the skin of this example is none other than an L-reg Metro diesel! The 1360cc engine sounds like a diesel but is at least allied to a decent 5-speed gearbox and, in action, is surprisingly sprightly. It's not an obvious choice and not one we'd readily promote because there are considerably more powerful units available within the Metro range. Still, for £500 it aptly demonstrates how cheaply a modern donor car can be bought. One point to remember is that the performance models don't only have better engines but also improved suspension, with uprated anti-roll bars and dampers.

The X21 doors open wide to give easy access to the interior, but they do feel a bit lightweight and lack any metal internal structure (other than what's required for the windows). Inside, Paul Banham's careful repainting of the internal surfaces has certainly done wonders for the otherwise mundane Metro interior. The big old Granada seats don't exactly feel sporty, but it's nice having leather instead of the velour that comes with even the top spec GTi models (although those seats give greater support).

On the move there's little disguising the scuttle shake evident through the steering. It's certainly not alarmingly vague but neither is it terribly pleasant. On better road surfaces it's largely forgotten but hit some poorer back roads and the reduction in structural rigidity is more obviously exposed. That said, it's not disastrous to the enjoyment of the X21, merely a demonstration of the limitations involved with this kind

Below: Diesel donor engine not an obvious choice although it works surprisingly well.

Below: Great detailing on the current car, with good use of mainstream light fittings.

Dave Reed has made a terrific job of his X21, especially considering its build cost of just £3500. Large boot is a big plus point for this practical roadster.

of body conversion. If you're looking for sports car handling and body control then the chances are you'll be disappointed – the X21 looks the part and handles, well...quite adequately.

Behind the front seats is the original bench seat which, as a result of being moved forward slightly, offers only small child seating capacity rather than for adults as in the Metro. Open the boot and the cavernous storage capacity has real value. Paul Banham's only too aware that the purse strings in most households are not usually held by the husbands, so getting the thumbs up from the ladies in an important aspect in the X21's appeal.

Protection from the elements is therefore of critical importance and the X21 has a very good looking soft-top arrangement with an excellent front locating method which promises a good weather-tight seal. It's also easy to put up and take down.

All told, the X21 looks sensational, the interior is comfortable and, with the right engine under the bonnet, it'll be reasonably quick. The conversion from Metro monocoque to Banham convertible is comparatively straightforward and the end product is acceptably rigid. Indeed, it's difficult not to like this car because it does what it is supposed to do extremely well. The X21 is a good laugh – so go on, enjoy yourself.

The customer car

Dave Reed is doing just that. His metallic blue X21 has been on the road for just a couple of months and he's clearly loving every minute. As a trained mechanic he was ideally placed to tackle the donor's bodywork modifications and special welding requirements, and it

Below: Rear seats get used, hence the seat belts. Right: MG Maestro wheels work well. Removable hard-top should give the car all-year-round practicality.

was the X21's simplicity and great looks that really appealed. But above all else, he couldn't justify having a kit car for occasional use and the X21 will be his daily runabout, taking him to and from work.

Having built a GP Spyder ten years ago when he and his wife Sue had more time on their hands, Dave knows what kit building is all about. But with two sons, Matthew (12 years) and Daniel (10 years), something with more than two seats was a priority. "I looked at the Quantum 2+2 and I liked it when it came out," remembers Dave, " but I think it is looking a bit dated now.

"I'd seen the Banham X99 and liked that. I'd never seen the X21 in the flesh but I'd seen photos on the internet and in magazines. I ordered the build video before I bought the kit and I liked the quickness of the build. I also spoke to Paul Banham a lot and the theory was that I would take a fortnight off work and do it in one hit."

First job was to find a suitable donor car, and a call to Paul Banham revealed that he was regularly at his local car auctions and he offered to keep an eye out for a suitable Metro. Not long after, the call came in that Paul had found a Metro and for £500 it was on a transporter and making its way to Dave's Bristol base. The H-reg 1.1S Metro looked perfect, with damage to the rear wing being the reason for its demise. Closer inspection revealed a few irritating problems, such as a knackered clutch, and Dave feels he might have got a slightly better deal had he looked around more carefully in his local area. Still, in most respects everything was in order, the interior being pristine and the shell itself largely devoid of rust.

Interior has been kept completely standard, including door cards and carpets.

Dave specifically avoided 16-valve engines and he's very happy with this K-series derived 1100cc unit. It means parts are cheap, too.

From the outset performance wasn't an issue and Dave specifically did not want a 16-valve Metro GTA or GTi engine. "I wanted a 1.1 or 1.4 8-valve," he explains. "I didn't want to go into 16-valves or fuel injection. I think they're over-rated. You get a bit more power if you're revving them but at town speeds an 8-valve is much better. Access around the engine is also improved and parts are cheap." As a car for daily use, the 1.1-litre K-series engine was perfect.

While a two-week build may have been optimistic, Dave had the donor stripped, roof chopped off and additional strengthening bars all in place within seven days. But both work and family commitments soon saw the project draw out from weeks into months, finally hitting the road after about four months of part-time work.

While Dave's mechanical knowledge meant he found the project easy, he feels he was also aided by the X21's essentially simple construction. "Mechanically you do so little," he comments. "I haven't even drained the radiator!"

Fitting the bodywork proved a question of trial fitting, trimming back the steel Metro extremities and then re-fitting – eventually everything was in place. Contrary to Banham's recommendations, Dave permanently fixed the bodywork in place prior to fitting the doors. While the doors themselves use all the original Metro hinging points there's only a limited amount of room for adjustment and where Dave had fixed the rear wings in place it became clear that he'd pulled them in just a little too far. The result is that the rear ends of the

In action the X21 feels well sorted and scuttle shake on this customer car is more controlled than on company demo. 1100cc engine also surprisingly capable.

doors don't quite line up as perfectly with the rear bodywork, although the side skirts go some way to hiding the error.

Elsewhere the build progressed easily, Dave using some concealed Vauxhall Vectra bonnet hinges for the X21 boot lid rather than the external ones seen on Banham's demo cars. Up front he also found he had to strengthen the bonnet corners in order to get them to match the shape of the main tub, since the standard bonnet flexed too much.

Paul Banham had persuaded Dave that he didn't want to have a coloured gelcoat finish and once all the panels were in place Dave could see why – the quality of finish wasn't high. Dave did all the bodywork preparation himself, before having the car professionally sprayed, and he found he had to do a lot of filling and smoothing down on the panels to get an acceptable finish. However, once painted in a terrific Vauxhall light metallic blue, all was forgotten – the X21 looked superb.

Back at home, the interior was quickly refitted and remains in completely standard form. Even the door cards simply pop straight into place on the new fibreglass doors. Outside Dave wasn't about to spend a fortune on fancy alloys and came across some MG Maestro wheels that fit perfectly – £100 and they were his.

Problems with Paul Banham's hood supplier led Dave to opt for the fibreglass hard-top which, conveniently, also happened to be cheaper! A very smooth looking design, the only problem has been finding and installing the Rover 200 rear glass. At over £150 new, Dave was keen to source a second-hand one, but wherever he went he was told that it was impossible to remove the glass from the donor's tailgate without damaging it.

Having found a suitable tailgate, he realised just how difficult it would be to get the glass out. The hard rubber trim that goes around the glass is bonded onto the glass before it is placed in the tailgate, so removing the glass is almost impossible without damaging the plastic surround. Having said that, Dave's managed it with only minor damage to the plastic edging which will in turn be largely hidden once fitted to the new Banham hard-top. Having kept the wiring for the Metro's heated rear window, he can simply plug it onto the hard-top whenever he uses it.

Initial impressions of Dave's car are extremely encouraging. The finish of the bodywork looks terrific and the alignment problems that Dave had with the doors will be largely missed by most onlookers. The X21 has a terrific production car feel to it and Dave's use of budget Maestro wheels works surprisingly well.

Despite having bog-standard Metro seats, carpets and dashboard, the interior is very acceptable and offers all the mod-cons that come with productions cars, such as comprehensive demisting and fresh air ventilation. If there's one area of the trim that lets this car down then it's the inner windscreen surround, which Dave did in a rush and knows full well that it looks...well, awful. When the opportunity arises it'll get changed.

Out on the road the X21 performs admirably and feels surprisingly rapid considering its 1100cc engine. The ride is also quite acceptable thanks to the addition of a small bag of sand which Dave's dropped into the spare wheel well. Prior to this technical addition the back of the car sat up a little too high and tended to skip about a bit on the road – there simply wasn't enough weight over the back wheels.

Dave's aware that there's a bit of scuttle shake but, as he rightly points out, it's no worse than a Mk2 Astra convertible and it appears a little better than the

Banham demonstrator. Indeed, everything about this car feels well sorted and we can easily see Dave using the car on a daily basis once the hard-top is painted.

But what about the all-important bank balance? "I was hoping to build it for what I could sell my Cavalier for," says Dave, "which is about £2200." But while they were fully prepared to hit £3000, Dave and Sue are perhaps a little disappointed that the final figure was almost exactly £3600. A quick add-up of the components reveals where the money has gone...

Stage 1 kit	£450
Sage 2 kit	£1170
Hard-top	£200
Lights etc	£450
Donor	£550
Paint	£400
Wheels	£100
Rear glass	£70
Anc. parts	£200
Grille mesh	£15
Windscreen	£50
Total	**£3655**

What's clear from this list is that no single item really bumped up the price while things such as the paint were found very cheaply indeed. Dave has certainly hunted around for a lot of items and made up a few bits himself, such as a bespoke rear silencer, so it's easy to see how this figure might go up by another £1000 if you weren't too careful.

Having said that, there aren't many kit cars that are genuinely practical for all-year use and which can accommodate two young kids in the back. Add in the X21's striking looks and the fact that it still comes in well below our £5000 threshold and we remain impressed.

Chapter Fourteen

Tempest

The company

Within *Budget Blasters* we've tried to show that it doesn't matter what style of car you're after, the kit car scene has something to satisfy everyone within our comparatively tight budget. But when you look at what we'd call the traditional roadster scene your options are not quite so varied. The big problem for us is that traditional roadsters tend to require a lot of fancy bolt-on goodies if they are to look convincing – lots of chrome or stainless steel, wire wheels, walnut dashboards, glinting instruments and good quality carpet and seats.

None of these things come cheap and it's all too easy to spend two or three thousand pounds just on finishing touches. Add in the fact that most traditional tourers will require painting (because while wings etc are in fibreglass, the bonnets tend to be in louvred aluminium) and we'd estimate that most cars within this marketplace tend to cost between £7500-£12,000. Not even close to our meagre £5000 budget.

But all is not lost, and the tiny Tempest roadster is one of just a very small handful of traditional tourers that we feel you could genuinely assemble with a tight bank account. While the car was originally launched in the late Eighties, it has essentially been in hibernation for the last ten years or so and has only recently been resurrected by new owner and long-time car enthusiast Steve Campbell.

"I've always been a practical person," says Steve. "At thirteen I was making push bikes, at fifteen I rebuilt a boat and at sixteen I decided I wanted to have a car of my own. I saw a Jensen 541R in a local service station for £300. I agreed to buy it, went home and phoned up the insurance company and they quoted me £1500 third

Within months of acquiring the project, Tempest Cars was back in the limelight.

Above: Steve Campbell is the man behind the relaunched Tempest.

112

party only. This was in 1969! Instead I bought an Opus HRF kit and built that."

The frankly bizarre looking Opus HRF opened Steve's eyes to the world of home-built cars and while he's not owned many kit cars since then, he's always kept a close eye on the scene. "I've always been involved with the car industry and I moved into automotive trim. I broke a bag of cement in the back of my wife's car when I was building a house and I found out that concrete doesn't come out of carpet. So I made a tailored liner for the boot – called it a Hatchbag, moved out of industry and started a small business making boot liners."

Despite being a huge success, the operation went belly-up in the Nineties' recession. Steve started from scratch again and everything was going smoothly until an order from a mainstream manufacturer was suddenly moved abroad. Having already invested in the machinery necessary to complete the promised work, it nearly went pear-shaped for a second time. But Steve managed to keep it together while promising himself that he'd never again have all his eggs in one basket.

"I wanted to get back to my passion, which was always cars," he continues. "I'd got a fibreglass moulding division, a metalworking division and a trimming division, so I had all the fabric to do everything. I found an advert in the back of *Which Kit?* magazine for a Jaguar XJ13 replica. I bought the moulds, had the chassis made, had a body made – it looked gorgeous but I started thinking 'who is going to buy this car?' It was a classic track car and I was having doubts about it."

By now Steve was once again dipping his toes into the specialist car market with other manufacturers. "We were involved with BRA – doing all their upholstery. We do the hoods for the Liege, did a lot of work with Mark Grinnall on the Scorpion three-wheeler, did a lot of development work with the Strathcarron and designed the soft-top for the new Jensen, which we still make."

By now he was becoming something of a three-wheeler fan and he bought as JZR for a bit of after-hours fun. Wondering whether manufacturing his own three-wheeler would be a commercial proposition, he visited the Stafford kit car show in 2000. "I chatted to George Reed of STATUS and the Liege team, which made me realise that the Reliant running gear was ideal. To learn more about the product, I bought an anorak and joined every Reliant Owners' Club that I could including, amongst others, the Reliant Kitten register."

Above: Interior on this customer-built example is terrific. Ultra simple dash really suits the car well.

It was to prove an inspired decision. "In the back of the first newsletter I received was an advert for the moulds and rights to the Tempest. I knew the car because a pall of mine actually owned the car you've tested. I used to see this thing every day and loved it – so when I saw the advert for the moulds I jumped in my van, drove up to Kendal and struck a deal with John Box, the previous owner."

By March of 2001 Steve was a fully-fledged kit car manufacturer, back at the Stafford kit car show, but this time with a car of his own. Not surprisingly, it hasn't all been plain sailing since then. When Steve began to assemble the first new car, he soon realised that the plans he had acquired were for the original company's

Tiny Reliant 850cc 4-pot tucked away in engine bay. Access not brilliant, but OK for general maintenance.

prototype, which just happened to be slightly smaller than the production kits that went out to the public.

Steve needed to get hold of an existing car from which he could take measurements and see the build process first hand. Not only did he find the completed example we were able to drive but he also bought a part-built car that was perfect for stripping back down and taking in-depth measurements from. "Everything is now on computer," explains Steve. "All the patterns, plans, drawings and components are all done on AutoCAD and all the brackets are now laser cut."

While a 4-wheeled Reliant Fox may not sound like an obvious donor car for a traditional tourer it offers a number of appealing features, not least the fact that the chassis and running gear are retained as standard. This not only endows the car with a relatively easy build but the retention of the chassis means the Tempest is exempt from the Single Vehicle Approval test that most kits cars must pass before they can be used legally on the road.

Because the Reliant is also tiny and very light, it means the Tempest is also very small and can make the most of the donor's diminutive 850cc engine. For those who hark back to Austin specials and other pre-war roadsters, the Tempest's teeny dimensions give it a unique advantage over most other traditional roadsters in the kit car market.

Of particular importance to us is the Reliant's other key appeal – it's very cheap to buy. Add in the fact that you retain so much of the donor and it means the Tempest is an extremely affordable project to build. "You couldn't spend more than £4500," says Steve, "and you can spend as little as £2500. You could even spend less than that because you don't have to buy my aluminium panelling – you could buy your own and cut up the sections yourself."

It's an appeal that hasn't been lost on his new customers and, while the Tempest is unlikely to sell in large volumes, those that take the plunge will have an interesting car that hasn't cost them a fortune. "I've been pleasantly surprised with the response, to be honest," comments Steve. "We have over 120 people currently on our database and twelve people building kits at the moment. We expect to exceed the original production run of 24 certainly by the end of 2002."

The company car

Base for any Tempest remains a 4-wheeled Reliant Fox, with virtually all of the mechanical components retained in largely standard form. That means a double wishbone front suspension, leaf-sprung rear live axle, drum brakes at each corner and an 850cc engine and 4-speed gearbox under the bonnet. A special adaptor bracket helps to lower the front suspension an inch or two, while the engine and gearbox are pushed further back and down into the original chassis (a ladderframe affair with central cruciform structure).

Onto the chassis is then bolted a tubular subframe for additional strength and onto this is located the bodywork. The latter is largely of aluminium, although the nosecone, front and rear wings, scuttle top and rear bumper panel are in fibreglass. While the test car is an original customer-built Tempest, new kits will also benefit from a fibreglass floor section instead of the heavier mild steel used in the originals, while new seats are in the pipeline and down in the footwell the pedal positions may yet be tweaked for a little more space.

Despite the test car being of the old Tempest variety, it's still a pretty good representation of what you can expect from the new owner. First impressions are of how small it is – it's tiny and that in itself will hold a great appeal. The styling is perhaps a tad 'toy-like' (and especially fussy around the rear fibreglass bumper section) but a decent period paint finish, tan interior and wire wheels all help to bring a suitably 'old-world' sense of occasion.

Open the door and slide onto the bench seat and you're once again reminded of just how small this car is – the cockpit is very snug. With the door shut you find yourself nicely supported on the inside by the fabricated armrest and on the outside by the inner door panel. The flat back of the bench-style seating is less supportive, while the inability to move the seat forwards or backwards would be a limiting factor if this were a factory trim kit. As it happens, Tempest is looking into making its own bucket seats.

With such a tiny cockpit it's important to keep everything as minimalistic as possible, and the tiny wooden dash binnacle (rather than full-width affair) is a lovely touch. Exposed demisting vents and piping on either side of the dash seem perfectly at home here, while a tiny centre console deals with heater controls

Below: Typical customer build details include the location of the knock-on wire wheel hammer.

Above: Standard Reliant front suspension works extremely well. Steering completely devoid of bumpsteer and even front drum brakes seem to work well.

and other ancillaries.

The driving position itself is surprisingly good and we weren't too fussed by the apparently narrow pedals. Even with a large Moto Lita steering wheel, there's plenty of room above your legs, and only the lack of a decent set of rear view mirrors reminds you of this car's obvious pre-SVA build. Inertia reel seatbelts are a pleasant surprise, while behind the occupants is a remarkably generous storage area which is capable of swallowing the semi-rigid side-screens when they're removed from the doors.

Open the centre-hinged bonnet and you'll notice just how small the Reliant 4-pot really is – resembling a shrunken A-series engine out of something like an Austin Healey Sprite. While there's plenty of room around the engine and its ancillaries, the centre-hinged bonnet and the engine's location right down in the bowels of the engine bay will make servicing more tricky than you might expect. Typical of a privately-built car, this Tempest has lots of nice touches in the engine bay, including a well located knock-on wheel hammer and jack.

All Reliant three or four-wheelers come with the same 850cc engine producing about 34bhp. With an all-alloy construction they're incredibly light and have an entertainingly free-revving nature. There is also a

Above: Bench seat doesn't adjust but driving position is good. Production kits will have option of in-house designed seats.

wealth of tuning knowledge regarding these popular little engines, although ultimate output is unlikely to be a priority for most Tempest customers.

In this customer car the engine starts cleanly on the manual choke while the underslung exhaust keeps the volume down to an eager thrum. The gearshift on this car seem rather vague, although the gears themselves are encouragingly close set.

On the move, the ride initially feels a bit firm, and this car uses the standard Fox 3-leaf springs rather than the more compliant single-leaf items found on the three-wheeler variants. After a short while it isn't such as issue and the Tempest's ride remains assured at all times.

Far more impressive is the complete lack of any scuttleshake – a familiar traditional tourer problem which is surprisingly absent here. In fact, you can hit some extremely unforgiving potholes and find virtually no unpleasant feedback whatsoever through the steering or scuttle. It's most impressive.

Drum brakes at each corner is one feature of the Tempest that is unlikely to inspire confidence but they appear to work admirably, if not quite with the control of a more modern front disc set-up. Of course, as with most kit cars, the drum brakes are hardly having to work very hard because the car itself weighs very little, so while converting to discs may be possible, it wouldn't be high up on our priority list.

Neither would any great hike in power. This largely standard engine benefits from a more free-flowing air-filter and other minor ancillary benefits (such as the exhaust) and it performs with entertaining enthusiasm. Nope, we're not saying that it is terrifically quick, but neither is it especially slow.

Much more important is the package as a whole. With such a sorted chassis, you can really get on and enjoy the Tempest. The engine is as endearing as we've always been led to believe (and it was this driver's first experience of the little 850cc unit). It's a real charmer, with bags of character.

Indeed, that's the feeling you come away with after a drive in the Tempest – it makes no pretence at being an out-and-out performance machine. This is a car in which to have some fun and it delivers that with great panache. From the intimate and distinctive interior to the terrific structural integrity and zingy engine and gearbox package, this car's a great hoot and it's easy to see why Tempest MD, Steven Campbell, has become so smitten with it.

As a build project, it looks as though the Tempest won't test you too much. The retention of the chassis and its suspension in largely standard form, along with the steering, cooling and electrical systems, should ensure the build is an easy one. The bodywork subframes simply bolt into place and the aluminium

Below: Boot space is surprisingly deep, easily swallowing removed side-screens.

bodywork comes pre-cut and with primary folds already in place.

If finding a suitable donor puts you off, then Tempest Cars is constantly on the look out for them and usually has a few suitable machines available for customers. Spares certainly shouldn't be a problem and, as we've already mentioned, tuning goodies are boundless.

The customer car

With the revitalised Tempest project still in its infancy, it was always going to be difficult to put our hands on a completed example, since all of the current kits are still in the midst of being assembled.

John Howell is one of the current crop of Tempest builders and he can't wait to get his car on the road later in the year. "I've never actually done a kit car before," he explains, "but I've had old Triumphs and things like that." A one-off visit to the Stafford show in 2001 saw him walk onto the newly launched Tempest stand. "I came across what to me looked like a 1950s sports car and I really liked the look of it. I didn't know what it was but it went from there."

While John was amazed when he heard what was under the traditional tourer lines, the humble underpinnings didn't put him off – if nothing else the car would be cheap to run! In the Tempest price bracket there didn't seem to be a great deal of competition, but John was also keen on three-wheelers. Despite these being within his budget, John felt that, for the money, the Tempest represented better value considering the potential to build a car for around £2000.

With his mind set, John spoke more with Tempest MD Steve Campbell and ended up buying a donor directly from him which had already been stripped of its old bodywork. All Reliant Foxes have galvanised chassis

Below: John Howell is currently in the midst of his Tempest project and looking for a sub £3000 build.

Tempest proves that traditional roadsters don't have to be expensive. Basic interior is the perfect starting point for a budget build.

and John removed all the suspension and cleaned the frame, which proved to be completely rot-free. For visual effect more than anything else, he gave the chassis a coat of primer before finishing it off with a gloss black topcoat.

Re-assembly of the rolling chassis was easy. "I was able to put a rope underneath the engine, manhandle it myself and lift it up and drop it into the frame," says John. "It's so easy to work on in that respect because everything is so very light." As the project stands at the moment, the body subframes have been bolted down and the aluminium and fibreglass body panels trial fitted.

John's already decided on a colour, dark metallic blue, and he's even bought the paint. "I'm going to do the spraying myself. I've only got a small compressor but it's only a small car. It's quite easy to do so long as you take your time." For the interior he's looking for something a bit special and his long-term association with various Triumphs means there's likely to be plenty of period wood finishings and no doubt a few chrome bezelled instruments. "Looking at a few kit cars that I've seen in the past, I think the interior always lets them down."

Under the bonnet, the 850cc engine has received a basic overhaul and John's not discounting the possibility of tuning at a later stage. "Obviously, it's not going to be any fireball away from the traffic lights, but they do race these engines and it's quite possible to tune them."

Looking forward, John doesn't see the build dragging on forever and he's not expecting any big frights when it comes to the budget. "I'd love to have it on the road this summer," he suggests. "I don't think that's completely out of the question but the weather's holding me up at the moment because I'm building it under a car port. Tempest says it's possible to build a car for under £2000 and I think it may be possible if you're inventive about saving parts and reconditioning them yourself – I think that's quite a viable proposition. Up to now I've spent about £1500. If you start adding weather gear that will put the price up but that's something you can do without. So to me it's an extra and I don't count that in the actual cost of getting the car on the road."

Up to now John has clearly been enjoying the build experience and is relishing driving the finished article. Only the lack of a decent build manual has caused any great headaches, but we suspect those will be long forgotten when he gets the Tempest on the road.

Chapter Fifteen
Sylva Striker

The company

Behind Westfield and Caterham, the Sylva Striker is one of the oldest Lotus Seven inspired replicas and it packs a competition punch that the young guns would die for. The Striker, along with its stablemate, the Mk4 Phoenix, has won the 750 Motor Club Kit Car Championship eight out of the last twelve years, with class wins in every single season since the series began in 1984! To say that Sylva has dominated the Championship is something of an understatement – it has simply set the standards by which others must try and follow.

Sylva Autokits was formed by structural design draughtsman, Jeremy Phillips, in 1981 but his hands-on car building experience began much earlier. "My brother built a special around an old Riley," remembers Jeremy, "and I was always champing at the bit to do that. I'd even started to build my first car when I was at school. It was pretty awful but I did get it on the road and it sort of grew from there.

"I've built various specials over the years and I've also built a couple of kit cars – a beach buggy and an Arkley. That's when I first met Nick Green [subsequent founder of NG Cars], because he was into Arkleys as well. I bought an MGB and started drawing up a chassis for it with a view to the two of us working together, but I got so busy with the drawing work and earning really good money that I got side-tracked. Nick went off and carried on with the MGB thing. I then decided that I wanted to do a much more contemporary car, which is what I did with the Sylva Star and Leader."

While the Star was only sold in limited numbers, it was the Vauxhall Viva-based Leader that really saw production numbers rise. And while Sylva's track expertise is well documented, these early cars were always conceived as road-going machines because, if nothing else, there was no race series for which they were eligible. But that was soon to change...

"In about 1982 *Cars & Car Conversions* magazine had a day at Mallory Park when they invited all the kit cars along," recalls Jeremy. "I took the Star with a

Top right: A little older and a little greyer, but Sylva's Jeremy Phillips is still designing some great affordable kit cars. Below: Here's the second Star ever to be made, back in 1982.

Above: Following the success of the Star, Sylva was quick to develop the Viva-based Leader.

1256cc Viva engine in it and I drove this thing around all day but nobody seemed to be interested in looking at it. Just as I was about to pack up, the magazine's editor Terry Grimwood came over and asked to have a drive. He did three laps and came in and said he couldn't believe the car. He subsequently wrote in the feature that he'd never driven a car with such good steering.

"From that event *CCC* decided to build one for the new kit car championship [which would start in 1984]. Terry Grimwood was on the front row of the grid in a Star at Brands Hatch for the first ever kit car race. You can imagine how fired up that made me. We could have won that race if a bloody plug lead hadn't fallen off – but that's the story of motor racing! As it was, it was a flipping Dutton which won – so Dutton had that privilege!"

1985 saw the Mk1 Striker hit the roads, powered by a rotary Mazda RX7 engine. Originally based in the New Forest in Hampshire (the company's logo is meant to signify the green New Forest trees and purple heather that surrounded the workshop), production moved up to Lincolnshire in 1987.

Throughout the company's development, the Striker has always remained the focus of attention, but Jeremy Phillips' creative mind has also found time to produce several other significant models. The Sylva Fury came about in 1991 and was an immediate success story, but by 1994 the project was sold on to Fisher Sportscars to make way for Sylva's next model, the Stylus (now with Specialist Sports Cars). Complete with doors, externally accessible boot (rather than from behind the seats) and a conventional bonnet design, the Stylus was a natural evolution of the Fury bloodline. But the company's next model, the Jester, was a big departure...

For starters, the 1996 Sylva Jester (now with Harlequin Cars and mentioned in Chapter 16) was front-wheel-drive, using the largely unmodified engine and suspension package from a Mk2 Ford Fiesta, but it was the styling that caused the most surprise. Rather than doing the styling himself, as he had on all his previous offerings, Jeremy called in graduate designer Huw McPherson who came up with the car's bold and downright wacky external shape.

Using the ageing Mk2 Fiesta meant that the Jester, like all of Jeremy's creations, was an extremely affordable project, and a typically capable chassis design ensured the car performed to a standard few

Below: Mazda rotary powered, this was the very first prototype for the Striker. Below right: GRP bonnet and rear wings now beginning to show more familiar lines.

Above: This one-off Mk1 Striker was the first kit car racer to be fitted with a rotary Mazda engine and was raced by Jeremy's brother Mark in the mid '80s.

would have given it credit for judging by its playful exterior. Continuing his association with the Ford Fiesta, Jeremy moved the engine and gearbox package to the back of his latest chassis to produce the mid-engined Sylva Mojo in 1999. Styled in-house, the new car was clearly back on the sports car trail and, with yet another superb chassis and suspension package, the Jester has thrilled all those who've managed to blag a drive. However, despite excellent reviews in all the press, the Mojo has not been one of the company's best selling models, leaving another car launched by the company in this same year to take the lion's share of orders, even outpacing the still popular Striker...

The redesigned Phoenix is an upgrade to the race-inspired Mk4 Clubmans which spawned the original Fury and it proves that Jeremy Phillips still has a knack for producing extremely pretty sports cars. Maintaining a simple, no-frills approach that has stood all Sylva's cars in such good stead, the Phoenix is devoid of doors, opening boot or even a full windscreen.

Of course, while all of these exciting new cars have been coming off the production line, the Striker has evolved with subtle tweaks to almost every area of its construction, from suspension components to interior design and fibreglass body mouldings. But forming the foundation of every car to come out of the Sylva workshop is a strong belief that all its products should be affordable, structurally well designed and offered in such a way that the home enthusiast is still free to introduce his own tweaks to the end product.

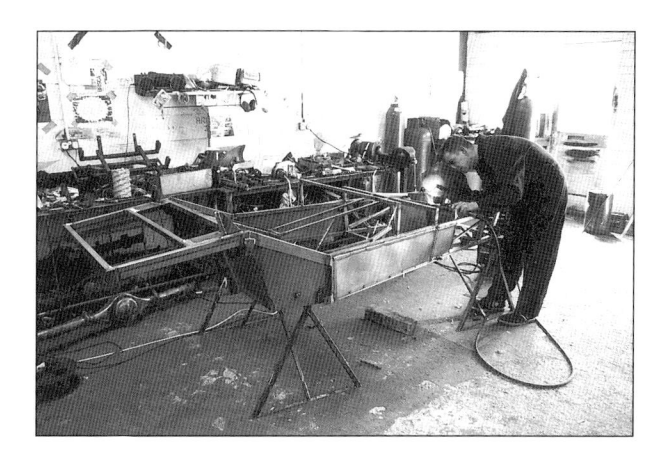

Above: A really good chassis design has always been the base for all Sylva models and has clearly helped the cars excel on the track.

"We're very much driven by price because we have to be," explains Jeremy. "If I was building something like a Formula Ford or Mallock, I could charge literally three times as much for the same amount of work. But I believe that the whole Lotus Seven inspired replica scene price structure is kept artificially low, so if you're going to play in that marketplace you've got to have a compatible price. I feel that what we do for the money is extraordinary."

But for all his reservations about the bargain basement prices dominating the Lotus Seven inspired market place at the moment, Jeremy has always believed in value for money. "I've always felt that the Sylva should be for the impecunious racer. He doesn't

Racing has always been central to Sylva's long-term success. Here's Jeremy at Mallory in '89, where the car won its class on its first outing.

Left: Latest model eyes up its forebears. Above: Extremely pretty Sylva Fury was launched in 1991 and was an instant success. Fisher Sportscars took it on in 1993.

want to go out and spent a bucket-load on a Vauxhall 16-valve. Some of my customers are doing it now – they'll buy a comprehensive kit for £4000, but their engine will cost £5000+. I think 'good grief, where's the logic in that?' I remember in my first race I used a 1300cc GT engine with a pair of Webers on it that must have cost me all of £100, and I had good fun with that."

While the factory demo car we drive in the next section is bike-engined, Sylva has always tried to make its demo cars representative of what an enthusiast might expect to achieve at home. "My latest demonstrator has a Pinto in it because it's a Sierra-based car and I feel obliged to present a demonstrator which reflects what half of my customers will do," says Jeremy. "The other half who will put in a Yamaha R1, Hayabusa or a Vauxhall 16-valve can still see what the potential is.

"But if you take a potential customer out in a car with a 170bhp Vauxhall in it, he knows he's only ever going to be disappointed when he installs his £150 Pinto. I can hand-on-heart say that the engine and gearbox in the new demonstrator cost £70 out of a Capri and it really goes well."

As for the track action, it still remains a vital element of Sylva Autokits' appeal. "I think it has been totally crucial," says Jeremy. "I don't do the shows and I don't think we could have survived without the motor racing." But while the company continues to reap the rewards of its racing success, Jeremy Phillips has had great fun personally campaigning his own cars in the mid-field. "Customers see me going along as a middle runner, having a bit of fun and without spending too much money.

"I often think that when other manufacturers decide they'll go kit car racing they only want to be on the front row of the grid. But they've missed the point really, because you just frighten people off if they think

Below and right: Sylva developed the Fury concept further with the Stylus, seen below in early buck form and (right) in productionised form.

122

Above: The author built this pretty Striker for Which Kit? *magazine in the early Nineties. The car featured a popular Striker engine – the 1600cc Fiat twin-cam.*

Above: Quirky Jester was full of neat ideas, including the almost standard use of Ford Fiesta running gear and engine.

that's the only place to be and they can't achieve it. Many people would love to try and don't mind running at the back of the grid – so long as they're out there and are actually doing it."

With sales of the Phoenix currently outstripping the Striker, Jeremy's wondering whether the tide is finally turning against the Lotus Seven inspired replica. "I suspect that if there's a significant change at the moment it's people getting a bit sick of all the Lotus Seven inspired replicas. The Striker fits in because it's different, but the Phoenix offers everything that the Seven can offer but looks fantastic on the road."

Track days are also having a big effect. "We're hardly selling any windscreens or hoods for cars," observes Jeremy. "I think the track days are probably responsible for it. They're maximum fun for not too much money."

So what about building a Striker on a really tight budget? What can one realistically expect from our self-imposed £5000 ceiling? While Jeremy would be the first to say it won't be easy, there are customers who've built superb examples for not much cash. "There was a really nice one built for about £3000 and he just selected the right bits at the right time. He probably bought his engine for about £200."

Indeed, as we've found throughout the process of producing this book, money is only part of the story when it comes to owning a car you can be proud of. "You don't have to spend a massive amount of money to build a nice car," says Sylva's Jeremy Phillips. "I've seen people spend a fortune and end up with quite an average car."

The factory car

The diminutive Sylva Striker makes almost every other car in the class look positively plump. And while there's little doubt that its styling is Lotus Seven inspired, it pushes the boundaries way beyond anything approaching a replica. It may be of that genre, but the

Mojo project continued Sylva's association with the humble Fiesta, this time locating the engine in the back for genuine sports car handling and ride.

Above: Most recent development at Sylva has been the re-introduction of an old favourite in the form of the Phoenix. Subtle styling upgrades along with no doors or windscreen make this a potentially cheap project.

Striker has always had a distinctive look that sets it apart from the melee of would-be Lotus impersonators.

The philosophy behind the Striker has always been to keep it simple and affordable and to that end it has

Below: The Striker as you'll find it today. This example was the company's first bike-powered car.

retained an Escort live axle rear suspension long after the rest of the field has moved onto Sierra-derived IRS set-ups. The company has shied away from modern twin-cams such as the Ford Zetec and Rover K-series (although customers have installed both) and instead almost single-handedly buoyed up demand for the 1300 and 1600cc Ford X-flows. Add in an almost unique enthusiasm within the industry for the old 1600 Lancia twin-cam lump and it's easy to see that Sylva has never followed the crowd but struck its own, highly individual path.

So when the current trend for installing bike engines into kit cars began a couple of years ago, Sylva was hardly about to jump on the bandwagon. But as what appeared to be a short-term fad developed into a genuine long-term innovation within the industry, even the Lincolnshire-based operation has had to rethink its strategy.

Rather than simply follow suit and bung in a Honda Fireblade engine (as a number of customers had already done), the company has typically looked at the concept afresh and come up with power options that have, to date, been ignored by the competition. The result is that the two cars you see here are fitted with a Honda CBR1000 water-cooled engine and a Suzuki Bandit 1157cc oil-cooled lump. The latter is owned by Sylva customer John Goodhand and his long-time experience with bike-engined autograss racers has been a big source of information to the factory.

The red factory-built demonstrator is the result but Sylva hasn't just stopped with the bike-installation, since this car is perhaps the most radical of any Striker to date. Even Sylva is coming to terms with the fact that Ford Escort donor components are becoming harder to source, so this car uses a new independent rear suspension set-up. Based around a Sierra differential, the system uses shortened driveshafts and the donor's bearing and brake system, all mounted on fabricated double wishbones, adjustable coil-over dampers and cast alloy uprights (fabricated items on production kits).

Up front a modified Sierra-based stub axle has replaced the modified Mk2 Escort item that has done the company proud for the last 17 years. Still using Sylva's long-standing and race-proven top swing arm, the new front set-up allows more of the single donor to be utilised, thus saving on scrapyard foraging and keeping costs to a minimum.

But it's at the back where the current car has really had to be completely redesigned to accommodate the new set-up. Allied to additional chassis bracing around the engine bay and modifications to the tunnel in order to accommodate a reverse box option, this chassis is quite different to anything we've seen from the company in the past.

For the bike installation, Sylva has followed a more tried and tested route of a lower engine cradle which is then rubber-mounted to the chassis. The company has then used a reverse box which is currently being used by its southern agent, Fisher Sportscars. As with most

Below: Ultra simple interior suits bike installation perfectly. Note bike instruments and switch gear.

Of just as much significance as the Honda CBR bike installation was this Striker's prototype full IRS rear suspension which has now been productionised.

of these units, it is mounted inside the centre tunnel, requiring a short prop back from the bike's gearbox before a longer prop takes drive back to the Sierra differential.

Keeping the Striker affordable has been a major concern, and it is one of the reasons why the company has opted for the CBR engine rather than the trend-setting Blade unit. At around £500 for the complete bike power package, this is considerably more affordable than the Blade, where prices are currently hovering around the £1100 mark. Not just that, but Sylva has retained the bike's instrument cluster and handlebar stalk controls.

Not that cost has been the only issue in choosing the CBR lump. The company hopes that the extra capacity of this unit over the 900cc Blade engine will make for a better road unit, with more torque and a longer life. That extra oomph should also make up for any shortfall in

Bare bones, balls-out fun!

actual power output compared to the modern superbike unit, while both feature 6-speed sequential gearboxes.

The new car certainly looks the part. A chopped-down windscreen follows the no-frills approach taken by existing competitors, while a wonderfully simple interior looks great with the CBR instrument cluster and separate warning light strip. The handlebar controls have been mounted on dedicated stalks and add to the fun. Sylva's standard trim package looks tight and fuss-free and the red gelcoat finish of the exterior bodywork looks well presented. Use of the Mojo's front cycle wings, with their angled front edge, also seems to suit the new car. The end result is an ultra simple-looking machine with a great single-minded focus.

First thing to strike you when you take the bonnet off is the size of the engine. While still small by production car standards, the unit is positively vast when sat beside a Blade installation. This is an older design and it just goes to show how the bike industry has moved on in recent years. Sylva has had to design a new air-box for the engine in order to keep it under the bonnet, but in most respects this is still a neat and tidy fitment.

Hop in and the Striker tucks in around you like a snug glove. These seats aren't designed to be adjustable, but the Striker's driving position has always seemed to be pretty perfect and this car is no different. It must be down to making racing cars – you don't win races in cars that are uncomfortable, and the Striker has a near perfect driving position without seemingly any requirement for adjustment.

Having retained the bike's ignition switch and stalk controls, just getting this car started requires no less than three switches to be thrown or pushed before the unit fires up. It's a good theft deterrent, since no self-respecting car thief would ever work it all out – not least because the gearbox must also be in neutral before anything happens. But when it does, there's no mistaking there's a bike engine under the bonnet.

As with most bike engines, it's push forward for first gear and then pull back to work your way on up through the cogs. Sylva's tiny gearstick seems too far from the steering wheel but you soon get used to it. The addition of the reverse box almost inevitably adds some mechanical noise to the whole operation so that low speed gear changes can be rather clunky. It is only when you start pushing on that everything seems to gel and the experience comes into its own.

There's little doubt that bike-engined cars have an all-or-nothing feel to them. Potter around town and none of them offer a very rewarding driving experience, but push on up into the higher revs and work at maximum performance and there's nothing quite like it

Difficult to see, but here's the double wishbone rear suspension exposed. Drum brakes help to reduce cost but not stopping potential.

John Goodhand's autograss racing experience made him an authority on bike engine use in 4-wheeled racers.

in terms of 4-wheeled fun. The engine noise is simply brutal while the gear changes suddenly become smooth and fluid – snapping up the sequential gearbox in a way that is simply impossible to replicate in a conventional car 'box.

At these moments the craze with bike engines makes perfect sense – this has a purity and single-mindedness that is utterly addictive. If nothing else, it delivers supercar performance for very little money. While the CBR engine may not officially match the Blade's 135bhp, out on the road you're unlikely to notice the difference. Whether it's the additional torque of this unit, or simply that telling the difference between 0-60 in 4.1 seconds or 4.8 seconds is pretty academic...who knows – this is almost certainly the quickest road-going Striker we've ever experienced.

But if the performance from the engine is impressive, then the new independent rear suspension is also something of a revelation. Strikers have always had a pretty firm ride in the past but the test car is transformed by the new package. Suddenly it makes the car less of a go-cart and more of a serious sports car. The Striker feels more settled than we remember it in the past, which is critical if you are to make fast progress on uneven back roads. Considering this machine's ultra light weight, the feat is all the more impressive, and this car hadn't even been fully set up when we drove it.

From our experience of the Sylva breed, this is about the purest Striker we've ever driven. The ultra simple exterior, lack of a windscreen, and the superbly trimmed interior with its bike instrument binnacle and warning lights all perfectly suit the tiny Striker's minimalistic approach.

As with all the bike-powered cars that we've driven to date, the installation will not suit everyone. Its total single-mindedness means this isn't a car for long weekend blasts across the country, but more for hour-long blitzes around your local lanes. For those who've already had a Lotus Seven inspired roadster, then the bike route makes perfect sense since it offers something quite new. But for kit car virgins, opting for a more conventional engine will almost certainly allow you more scope to enjoy your car on a regular basis. Of course, if track days are your thing, then you need look no further.

In terms of more conventional engines, then common sense would suggest that the Sierra donor car's 2-litre Pinto is the perfect option. In the teeny Striker it'll give superb performance even in largely standard form, while with a couple of Weber carbs on

By retaining some cheaper donor alloys and doing as much as possible himself, John managed to keep the cost of his car (in the background) to within our budget... just.

*Above: Interior uses Sylva's SVA spec dashboard.
Above right: 1157cc Suzuki Bandit engine gives good performance for the road.*

the side you'll really have a hooligan on your hands.

Not surprisingly, the specification of the factory demo car, with its fancy alloys and bike installation, up the build cost beyond our budget, and Sylva estimates that the private builder could assemble a CBR-powered Striker to the spec you see here for around £7000. Interestingly, the customer's Bandit-engined car has been completed for just £5500, so perhaps this is one company estimate that we can actually say is pessimistic rather than optimistic.

Since our test the company has produced new body moulds (and a new demo car) for the front bonnet which is now split into two panels – a fixed nosecone and more conventional removable bonnet section. Not only does it look better, it certainly makes removal of the bonnet considerably easier.

The customer car

Having built autograss racers for his two sons, John Goodhand felt it was time he did something for himself! Having followed the kit car industry for many years, he was aware of the major players, but his desire to use a bike engine meant he was largely restricted to the Lotus Seven inspired brigade. He did a reasonable amount of research, visiting Westfield (too expensive and too bulky), Tiger Racing (good but too expensive) and looking into the Locost (didn't like it at all). Having heard good reports about the Sylva Striker, he was impressed with the racing heritage and the price was also about right.

John bought a base chassis and body pack – opting for Sylva's lightweight racing body option to gain extra weight savings. Since the factory hadn't designed the IRS rear suspension at the time, John's car is Escort based and he's converted the rear axle to discs instead of the original drums.

For the engine he went for the Suzuki Bandit 1157cc engine with its 5-speed sequential gearshift. Having used the engine in his autograss racers, he knew of its strength and power (around 140bhp). Like Sylva's demo car, John also fitted a reverse gearbox but he's not convinced he'd do the same again.

John's car went through SVA in November 2000, initially failing on an exhaust radius and a hazard warning light in the wrong place. Future changes include fitting a decent steering wheel, some different wing mirrors and eventually replacing the Capri 4-spoke alloys. An all-up cost for the project is just over £5500, which seems quite amazing value considering the performance potential of the car. Although not quite within our strict budget, with the removal of the reverse gearbox (which John feels is a waste of time) he'd be under our threshold.

Unlike the autograss racers, this one is strictly for road use and occasional track days. Interestingly, John trailered the car over to Sylva, rather than drive it, and then used a full bike crash helmet when giving us a demonstration of its potential. While he loves the car, it aptly demonstrates the limitations of the bike installation in terms of everyday long distance use.

While Sylva's demo car uses an aftermarket car silencer, John Goodhand's Bandit-powered machine retains a bike box and it sounds absolutely superb. With a complete lack of even a basic wind deflector it's easy to see why John sticks with the helmet, because buffeting in his car is quite severe, even with a decent set of goggles in place. It certainly shows the value of a basic deflector such as that fitted to the factory demo car. But otherwise this was a storming performance, with brutal acceleration and a typical bike-induced adrenalin rush – all for a measly £5000.

Chapter Sixteen

Others to consider

Highlighting ten kit cars, even as varied as our selection, only tells part of the story because there are many other kit car manufacturers out there which are worthy of your consideration and which produce kits that can be built within our budget. In some cases these may be very small operations producing slightly quirky machines at the rate of just a handful a year, but others are big companies churning out the product in large volumes. As we've hopefully already demonstrated, it doesn't matter what style of kit car you're after, there's almost certainly something that fits the bill.

Of course, it's almost impossible to be absolutely comprehensive here, since some companies are so small we've perhaps forgotten they exist, while others may have products which we simply weren't aware could be produced within our £5000 budget.

LOTUS SEVEN INSPIRED REPLICAS

Formula 27

Contact: *Unit 6, Hope Mills Business Centre, Brimscombe, Stroud, Glos GL5 2SE.*
Tel: 01453 886223.
Website: *www.formula27.com*

Description: Having originally offered a basic plans-built kit, Formula 27 now only works on a conventional factory supplied body chassis unit. Still, using the Escort live axle and sourcing components competitively, you can still get on the road for within our budget. Aluminium side panels and rear bodywork give an authentic feel and the car has always performed admirably. More recently the company has specialised in more developed 'bike-engined offerings, but don't forget this budget version.

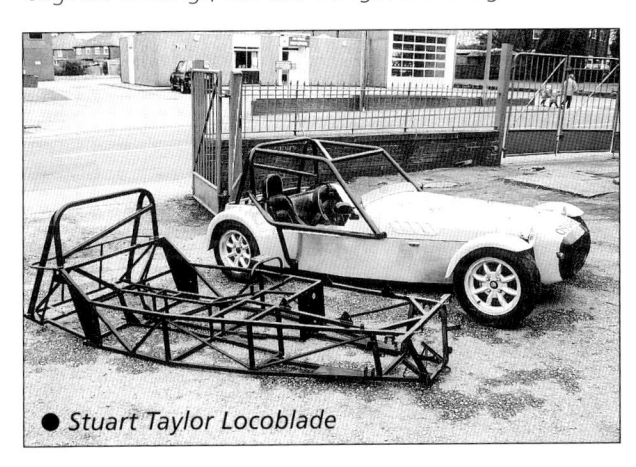

● *Stuart Taylor Locoblade*

Stuart Taylor

Contact: *1A West End Street, Stapleford, Nottingham NG9 7DA. Tel: 01159 399497*
Website: *www.stuart-taylor.co.uk*

Description: A product that has grown out of the Locost phenomenon, the Stuart Taylor Locoblade is one version pushing upwards in terms of cost and specification. Basic chassis is still an option but conventional body/chassis kits are now the norm. Locoblade uses the Honda Fireblade bike engine while Locorage has been

● *Formula 27*

● *Vindicator Sprint*

129

developed by Raw Engineering for use with the powerful and pretty Toyota MR2 twin-cam engine. LocoXflow is most conventional Ford Escort-engined machine and Stuart Taylor can offer factory built cars from £7500. The company has been very successful supplying cars for the popular 750MC Locost Race Series

Vindicator Sprint

Contact: *Unit G, Leona Industrial Estate, Nimmings Road, Halesowen, West Midlands B62 9JQ. Tel: 0121 602 1459*
Website: *www.vindicator.co.uk*

Description: While the Vindicator Sprint isn't strictly speaking a Lotus Seven inspired replica, it's definitely in that vein. Styling is a little bit agricultural but the driving experience is very good indeed. This is a larger car, offering more internal space than others, and it comes with independent rear suspension as standard, being largely Sierra based. A lockable boot is a bonus while the factory can offer some funky metallic gelcoat colours if the fancy takes you. Original swept wing design is available but cycle wings are the norm. Vindicator has been under new ownership since around 1999 and now has a much higher profile within the industry, with regular show appearances.

BWE Locust

Contact: *BWE Sports Cars, 13 Knowsley Street, Barnsley, South Yorkshire S70 6ET. Tel: 01226 293717*

Description: The plans-built Locust is one of the industry's older names and has recently been acquired by BWE Sports Cars. Based around a simple ladder chassis and, most significantly, a marine grade plywood monocoque body structure (trimmed externally in ultra thin sheets of aluminium), this is a great option for those with a degree of skill to produce something a bit different. We've seen some really immaculate Locusts over the years, largely based around Mk2 Escort mechanicals with X-flow engines. Wooden structure is surprisingly rigid, although a bit heavy for ultimate handling and performance. New fibreglass option will cure that, however.

Falcon LX4

Contact: *The Falconry, West Cranmore, Somerset BA4 4QS. Tel: 01749 880021*
Website: *falconcarsltd.co.uk*

Description: 4-wheeled version of three-wheeler. See later section.

TRADITIONAL ROADSTERS

Deauville Canard

Contact: *Deauville Cars, 3 Alleyne Way, Elmers Sands, Bognor Regis, West Sussex PO22 6JZ. Tel: 01243 586805*
Website: *www.deauvillecars.com*

Description: The quirky Deauville Canard is a wonderfully bizarre traditional tourer that uses a Citroen 2CV for its donor components. While the styling is definitely a little strange, it has a certain charm to it and early indications are that this newcomer has already found several customers. Quality of the mouldings appears to be good and the simple mechanical package should make for a relatively easy build, although the 2CV parts will inevitably require a degree of refurbishment. Big bonus is, of course, the relative affordability of this car, with completed examples able to hit the road from just over £3000.

● *Deauville Canard*

Marlin Sportster

Contact: *Marlin Cars, Mill Street, Crediton, Devon EX17 1EZ. Tel: 01363 773772*
Website: *www.marlincars.co.uk*
Description: There aren't many traditionally styled roadsters that fall into our tight budget, but Marlin

● *BWE Locust*

● *Marlin Sportster*

tells us that the Sportster will manage it if based around the company's all BMW-based kit package. Remarkably, this seemingly upmarket version of the Sportster actually uses more of the donor components than the existing Ford based car and, as such, can be built for less. However, don't expect much change from your £5000 but what you can expect is dynamite performance, superb kit quality and a car that really performs.

THREE-WHEELERS

Lomax 223

Contact: *Victoria Works, Maypole Fields, Cradley, Halesowen, West Midlands B63 2QB.*
Tel: 01384 410910.
Website: *www.lomaxmotorcompany.co.uk*

Description: If the popularity of three-wheelers has grown in the last few years, it's fair to say that Lomax was doing it before just about anyone else. The 223 has sold in simply vast quantities both in the UK and, most significantly, on the Continent. Simple Citroen 2CV engine and suspension is a winning formula while those on a really tight budget can even use the 2CV's original chassis – although older examples are inevitably rusty. Lomax offers all manner of upgrades, while the Lomax Lambda is the real quality item, with new front suspension design and a considerably more developed fibreglass body (all of which pushes the budget up towards our limit compared with the standard 223, with is very, very affordable).

● *Lomax 223*

BRA CX3

Contact: *Unit 14, Manor Industrial Estate, Flint, Flintshire, North Wales CH6 5UY.*
Tel: 01352 781773
Website: *www.bra-cars.com*

Description: Having recently sold on two of its three-wheeler models to the Leighton Car Company, BRA can now concentrate on the very pretty CX3. Based around its own suspension set-up and using a bike engine (Honda CX500 is a firm favourite) this is one car that has superb performance and great handling. Lots of fun, it may push our budget.

● *Falcon LX3*

Falcon LX3

Contact: *The Falconry, West Cranmore, Somerset BA4 4QS. Tel: 01749 880021*
Website: *www.falconcarsltd.co.uk*

Description: Fancy a Lotus Seven inspired replica, but with only one wheel at the back? Well here's your answer! Actually, the Falcon is also available with four wheels but this quirkiest of lookalikes doesn't stop there. Despite it's speedy styling, this is yet another three-wheeler which makes excellent use of the Citroen 2CV as a donor, this time complete with its chassis. Wood and steel side panels are skinned in aluminium to give it a period feel while the styling is surprisingly accomplished. Of course, the one thing that this Lotus Seven inspired machine lacks is the punch to back up its looks. Buy hey, it's extremely cheap and falls well within our budget.

Leighton & CV3

Contact: *Leighton Car Company, 6 Mill Lane, Coxheath, Nr Maidstone, Kent ME17 4HF.*
Tel: 01622 743358
Website: *www.bra-cars.com*

Description: Now under new ownership having been purchased from BRA Cars (the new company still using BRA's website at the time of going to press), both the Leighton and CV3 offer budget three-wheeled mayhem. The Leighton is an all-fibreglass bodied car with a bespoke chassis which uses Citroen 2CV components. However, the rear swing arm is a modified Metro item and the front suspension arms now benefit from new coil-over dampers to give improved handling. By comparison, the Citroen 2CV-based CV3 retains the donor chassis and features largely aluminium bodywork over an upper subframe. Both cars are cheap to build, the Leighton feasibly on the road for just £2000.

● *Tri-Tech Schmitt*

Tri-Tech

Contact: *Unit 1, Cuerden Green Mill, Sherdley Road, Lostock Hall, Preston, Lancs PR5 5LP.*
Tel: 01772 468317

Description: Pushing our budget to the limit are the ultra pretty Tri-Tech Zetta and Schmitt, replicas of a BMW Isetta and Messerschmitt KR201 respectively. Authentic sized motorbike engines ensure these wacky machines sound and go as well as the originals and the details are certainly spot-on. In all honesty, you'll probably struggle with our budget, but with real care and a decent slice of imagination, you might just manage it.

JZR

Contact: *Tel: 01254 760620*

Description: Is this the prettiest three-wheeler on the planet? Quite possibly. With more than a passing similarity between it and the considerably more expensive Triking, the bike-engined JZR is a real beauty. Out of production for a number of years, the JZR has almost been forced back into production by the demand for further kits. Engine options have varied considerably over the years, but regular appearances are made by the Honda CX500 unit and various Motor Guzzi and Harley Davidson lumps – bags of character and loads of fun. More adventurous engines will stretch our budget.

● *Free Spirit*

Free Spirit

Contact: *129 Hay Green Road, Terrington, St. Clement, Kings Lynn, Norfolk PE34 4PU.*
Tel: 01553 829761

Description: Here's a highly distinctive three-wheeler that has been around for many years although it's now only produced in very small numbers. The Free Spirit (and Kindred Spirit 2-seater) is a modern styled three-wheeler which uses a Renault 5 for a donor. Compared with a 2CV, the Renault engines makes this a real flyer, while Gordini performance variants are seriously quick. Handling is good and the little single-seater Free Spirit remains the most appealing of the lot in terms of styling and, quite literally, individuality. Having a gear stick between your legs is also interesting!

Pembleton Super Sports

Contact: *Pembleton Motor Co, Church House, Bayton, Kidderminster, Worcs DY14 9LP.*
Tel: 01299 832944

Description: Like so many kit car models, the Pembleton Super Sports was originally built for its instigator as a one-off. Then a few friends asked if they could have one and so it has gone on. The Pembleton is familiar in that it uses the Citroen 2CV for suspension and engine and unfamiliar in that its body is fabricated completely from aluminium sheet. Bodywork is not supplied pre-formed (unless you ask for it this way) and is fabricated by the builder over the metal framework beneath. Styling is ultra traditional and the car can be built very cheaply.

FUN CARS

RV Dynamics Bugrat

Contact: *56 Feering Hill, Feering, Colchester, Essex CO5 9NL. Tel: 07802 813649*

Description: There's much to admire about the RV Dynamics Bugrat, although perhaps the styling isn't to everyone's taste! Originally called the SV2000, the Bugrat is immediately distinctive because of its Skoda base. The Bugrat uses as much of the donor as possible and in largely unmodified form. Not surprisingly, the ultra cheap donor makes this an exceptionally affordable project and well within our budget. Chunky styling isn't as successful as some on the market but is more than made-up for by solid engineering and high quality mouldings. An ideal project for the first time builder.

Onyx Bobcat

Contact: *Becklands Cottage, Barnoldby Le Beck, Grimsby DN37 0AS. Tel: 01472 827813*

Description: Not many kit cars make use of the A-series engined Metro as a donor, but the Onyx is one of them. Also available as a three-wheeler, this is a super-cheap project with a real back-to-basics appeal. The styling is quirky to say the least but we've seen some well finished examples that look great fun. Performance can be brisk and the handling is apparently spot-on, while a K-series engined example is also being offered for those on a greater budget.

NCF Blitz

Contact: *Whittington Mill, Great Whittington, Newcastle upon Tyne NE19 2HU.*
Tel: 01388 526917
Website: *www.ncfblitz.freeserve.co.uk*

● NCF Blitz

Description: The Blitz is available in two forms, one a rear-wheel-drive funster and one a more purposeful 4x4 machine. The former is based around Mini donor parts and drops the A-series engine in the back to produce a mid-engined off-road buggy which can and has been converted by existing customers for road use (including SVA). The Blitz looks great and goes like hell on the dusty stuff. The Blitz 4x4 uses a Suzuki SJ chassis and running gear and, as such, avoids SVA by coming under the classification of a body conversion. Strange styling still has a chunky appeal and both can be completed for peanuts.

Scamp

Contact: *Scamp Motor Company, Crawley, West Sussex RH10 4NL. Tel: 01342 715088*
Website: *www.scampmotorcompany.co.uk*

Description: While the company is best known for its Mini-based funster, the little car went to the scrapyard in the sky once the powers of Single Vehicle Approval came into force. No less than 4000 Scamps had been produced by that time, but it's unlikely that the company's newest incarnation of the car will quite manage those figures. That said, the new Suzuki SJ or Daihatsu Fourtrak-based Scamp still offers a whole heap of 4-wheel-drive fun for very little money. Secret of this car is that it retains the donor's chassis and thus escapes the clutches of SVA.

Fereday Vario

Contact: *Fereday Cars, Hazeley Bottom, Hampshire RG27 8LX. Tel: 01252 845002.*
Website: *www.feredaycars.co.uk*

Description: Perhaps placing the Vario under the Fun Car category is unfair, because this car could be a practical everyday workhorse in pick-up format or, in more conventional car configuration, an appealing sports car. And that's half the appeal of this car, where the rear bodywork is offered in a number of different formats to suit different uses. Under the slick styling is a largely unmodified Fiat Uno engine and suspension package. Indeed, this really is a one-donor kit package, with absolutely everything salvaged from the single source. Fereday is confident that completed examples should be completed for under £5000.

YKC Pace

Contact: *Elvington Trading Estate, Elvington, York YO41 4AR. Tel: 01904 608899*
Website: *www.ykcsportscars.co.uk*

Description: YKC is marketing the newly acquired Pace alongside its traditionally styled roadsters, and the car is clearly aimed at those after a bit of fun on a budget. Having said that, you'll need to be careful with the pennies, since this car is designed for a Ford Zetec engine mounted amidships behind the driver. Suspension is largely bespoke, although main donor components are found on the Ford Fiesta Mk3. Styling has been improved recently after the removal of a rather cumbersome full roll-over cage that made it look like a stock car.

SPORTS CARS

Autotune Gemini

Contact: *Riverside Industrial Estate, Rishton, Blackburn, Lancashire BB1 4NF. Tel: 01254 886819*
Website: *www.kitsnclassics.com*

Description: The Gemini has almost certainly been in production longer than any other kit car described in this book. Its pretty styling harks back to the Elva of the 1960s and today the Gemini uses components sourced from either the Ford Escort or Sierra. The car has been developed over the last few years to make it even easier to build but it remains a kit car that responds well to builder input. We've seen some really great Geminis in the past and they certainly work well on both the road and track. Don't expect much change from our budget but you'll have a pretty car at the end of it.

Midas Gold Convertible

Contact: *Midas Cars, 14 Weights Lane, Redditch B97 6RG. Tel: 01527 584000*

Description: Midas has recently changed hands and the new owner is promising a rather higher profile for the product than has been seen in the past. The Gold Convertible is one of the more professionally styled kit cars on the market while its largely standard Metro underpinnings help it to remain an affordable project. A lockable boot, removable hard-top and roomy interior make it a very practical proposition while its front engined, as-per-the-donor layout makes for an easy assembly and hassle-free running. You'll be a little pushed on our budget, but it seems perfectly feasible to produce a terrific example for the money.

Vindicator Vulcan/Shadow

Contact: *Unit G, Leona Industrial Estate, Nimmings Road, Halesowen, West Midlands B62 9JQ. Tel: 0121 602 1459*
Website: *www.vindicator.co.uk*

Description: The Vulcan uses the same acclaimed chassis and suspension package used on the Sprint, so you're guaranteed a car that feels solid and which rides and

● *Vindicator Vulcan*

performs admirably. The all-enclosing bodywork of the Vulcan is, like the Sprint, a bit ungainly but it makes for a more practical design that also gets away from the endless Lotus Seven inspired replicas. The Shadow is a considerably more developed machine, with full doors and a much more productionised interior specification. The Shadow will probably push our budget but the Vulcan should be perfect.

BODY KITS

Paul Banham

Contact: *Unit 14, Castle View Business Estate, Gas House Road, Rochester, Kent ME1 1PB. Tel/Fax: 0181-289 0699*
Website: *www.banmoco.ndirect.co.uk*

Description: Paul Banham Conversions has given the body conversion business a new found urgency over the last few years, with a raft of new and diverse models using all manner of different donors. From the Mini-based Sprint (a Frogeye Spite replica), Skoda-based Spyder (a Porsche 550 Spyder replica!) to the MG Maestro-based (yes...really!) 200 (an RS200 replica) there's something for everyone here. However, it's the Metro-based X21 and Superbug that take the lion's share of sales. Welding skills will help here but prices are appealing, to say the least.

● *Banham Superbug*

Dakar

Contact: *Dakar Cars, 1 Rowhill Cottages, Puddledock Lane, Wilmington, Kent DA2 7QF.*
Tel: 01322 614044
Website: *www.dakar.co.uk*

Description: Based around a Range Rover donor, you wouldn't expect this to feature in the sub £5000 bracket but it certainly does. Rusty Range Rovers can be had for not much money and you throw away the old bodywork and drop on this chunky new GRP body for a serious semi-military look. Because the Dakar uses the Range Rover's chassis and running gear it can avoid SVA, while its reduced overhangs front and back make it a formidable off-road tool. Dakar Cars can always provide suitable donor cars (having loads in its yard every time we visit), so this could easily be a one-stop-shop project.

BUGGY MANUFACTURERS

GT Buggy

Contact: *PO Box 966, Portslade, Brighton BN41 2GL*
Tel: 01273 430505

Description: GT Mouldings has simply vast experience of the buggy scene and is run by buggy devotee and author on the subject, James Hale. The company owns a number of buggy moulds for such slices of history as the Manta Ray, Renegade, Bugle and Kyote. But it's the company's own brand new buggy that is the production mainstay, the GT Buggy. Launched in 1997 this brand new buggy is cunningly designed to retain the authentic buggy feel while using an unmodified VW Beetle floorpan – saving on the expense and expertise needed to shorten a floorpan for most buggy kits. Around £3000 should see you on the road, with

● *Dakar 4x4*

no SVA to worry about and, potentially, no road tax if you use the right donor car.

REPLICAS

Paul Banham Conversions

Contact: *Unit 14, Castle View Business Estate, Gas House Road, Rochester, Kent ME1 1PB.*
Tel/Fax: 0181-289 0699
Website: *www.banmoco.ndirect.co.uk*

Description: It's very difficult to build an authentic looking replica within our budget, but Paul Banham Conversions' body kits offer one of the few solutions. As outlined elsewhere in the chapter, the company does a large number of body kits, including replicas of a Porsche 550, Frogeye Sprite and Ford RS200. Welding skills will be a big bonus here since you'll be cutting up the donor cars and welding in new sections to maintain strength and allow fitment of the new bodyshells. The end products can look quite convincing and, with affordable tuning options, can even be made to perform reasonably well.

Appendix A

Contact Details

Blackjack Cars
Unit 5, Water-Ma-Trout Industrial Estate, Helston, Cornwall TR13 0LW.
Tel: 01326 574464. Website: www.oakes.co.uk

Fisher Sportscars
Unit 4, Underlyn Industrial Estate, Underlyn Lane, Marden, Kent TN12 9BQ.
Tel: 01622 832977.
Website: www.fishersportscars.co.uk

JAS Speedkits
Whispering Chimneys, Iwerne Minster, Dorset DT11 8LE.
Tel: 01747 812251. Website: www.beachbuggies.co.uk

MK Engineering
Unit 10 Harrison Drive Industrial Estate, Langold, Worksop, Notts S81 9RL.
Tel: 01909 731187.
Website: www.m-keenan.freeserve.co.uk

Paul Banham Conversions
Unit 14, Castle View Business Estate, Gas House Road, Rochester, Kent ME1 1PB.
Tel/Fax: 0181-289 0699. Website: www.banmoco.co.uk

Locost
Build Your Own Sports Car is available through Haynes Publishing, Sparkford, Nr Yeovil, Somerset BA22 7JJ. Alternatively, contact Locost Car Club, 1 Highfield Drive, Garforth, Leeds LS25 1JY.
Website: www.locostcarclub.co.uk

Robin Hood Engineering
Oxclose Lane, Mansfield Woodhouse, Notts NG19 8DF.
Tel: 01623 422286.
Website: www.robinhoodengineering.co.uk

Sylva Autokits
36 Station Road, Bardny, Lincolnshire LN3 5UD.
Tel: 01526 399401. Website: www.sylva.co.uk

Tempest Cars
Unit 2D Odyssey Centre, Corporation Road, Birkenhead, Merseyseide CH41 1LB.
Tel: 0151 652 3010. Website: www.tempestcars.com

Tiger Racing
Ecco New Toll Service Station, Thorney Toll, Nr Wisbech, Cambridgeshire PE13 4AX.
Tel: 01733 271131. Website: www.tigerracing.com

See **Chapter 16** for contact details of the other kits we feel could be built for under £5000

Appendix B
Show Dates

This is not intended to be a comprehensive list of kit car show dates, merely to detail those more established annual events and the month in which they occur. Phone the organisers for accurate dates and always make sure that the manufacturer you hope to see will definitely be in attendance.

MARCH

Car Craft
Location: Stafford County Showground, Stafford
Organiser: Limelight Exhibitions. Tel: 01737 225857.
Website: www.limelight-exhibitions.co.uk
Summary: Great season opener with good cross-section of manufacturers, large accessory support, dedicated cars for sale area and outside club stands.

APRIL

The European Kit Car Show
Location: Kent County Showground, Detling, Kent
Organiser: European Show Promotions. Tel: 01233 713878.
Website: www.car-shows.co.uk
Summary: Long running, mid-size event with generally good support from the kit car industry, reasonable club presence and 100s of privately owned cars.

MAY

The National Kit Car Motor Show
Location: National Agricultural Centre, Stoneleigh, Warwickshire
Organiser: Grosvenor Exhibitions. Tel: 01775 712100.
Website: www.grosvenor-publishing.co.uk
Summary: The big event of the year. If the weather is good, expect 1000s of privately owned cars to fill the vast club area while inside virtually all of the industry usually attends.

JUNE

The Alternative and Kit Car Show
Location: Newark and Notts County Showground, Newark on Trent, Notts
Organiser: Newark Promotions. Tel: 01526 320721.
Website: www.kitcarshow.co.uk
Summary: Major club event that has seen manufacturer attendance dwindle in recent years. Lots of special features going on outside but check first to see whether a specific manufacturer will be there.

The British Sports Car Festival
Location: Brooklands Museum, Weybridge, Surrey.
Organiser: Limelight Exhibitions. Tel 01737 225857.
Website: www.limelight-exhibitions.co.uk
Summary: Annual sports car event now redeveloped to include kit cars. A unique atmosphere is guaranteed at this historic British circuit. Absolutely loads to see!

JULY

Wheels Extravaganza
Location: Hickstead Showground, Sussex
Organiser: Limelight Exhibitions. Tel 01737 225857.
Website: www.limelight-exhibitions.co.uk
Summary: Staged on a single day, this low-key event is being redeveloped in 2002 to include hot rods and Japanese performance cars. No official manufacturer attendance, but a huge number of kit cars and other interesting machines in attendance.

SEPTEMBER

The National Kit and Performance Car Show
Location: Exhibition Centre, Donington Park Racing Circuit, Castle Donington, Derbishire
Organiser: Limelight Exhibitions. Tel: 01737 225857.
Website: www.limelight-exhibitions.co.uk
Summary: Massive manufacturers' support makes Donington one of the season's highlights. With kit cars allowed on the famous circuit (along with manufacturer test drives), this is also a unique opportunity to see the cars in action. Also expect a big club turnout.

NOVEMBER

The Great Western Kit & Sports Car Show
Location: Westpoint Exhibition Centre, Exeter, Devon
Organiser: European Promotions. Tel: 01233 713878.
Website: www.car-shows.co.uk
Summary: A superb curtain call for the season with good manufacturer support. Weather can occasionally affect outside displays, but they still turn up.

Appendix C

Accessory Directory

Here are all the accessory companies you may find of use in a typical budget kit car build.
If anyone is missing, it's simply because we forget them or didn't know they existed!

DONOR PARTS SUPPLIERS

Abbey Transmission Services (Ford axles/gearboxes) – Unit 15, Sidings Industrial Estate, Hainault Road, London E11 1HD. Tel: 0208-558 4028. www.abbeytrans.co.uk
Donor Spares (Ford) – 01473 272950
Eddie White Motorsport (Ford) – 48 Evershill Lane, Morton, Alfreton, Derbyshire DE55 6HA. Tel: 01773 875105
Ian Harwood Ltd (Ford) – Capernhurst Lane, Whitby, Ellesmere Port, South Wirral, Cheshire L65 7AQ. Tel: 0151 339 2801
Kit-Fit (largely Ford packages) – 01636 893453
Viking Co (Rover) – Tel: 0121 459 6866

ENGINE SPECIALISTS

Cheshire Motorcycle Salvage – Tel: 01625 502372. www.cheshiremotorcyclesalvage.com
DJE (Rover V8) – Tel: 0247 6352888. www.djev8.com
Eddie White Motorsport (Ford & Vauxhall) – 48 Evershill Lane, Morton, Alfreton, Derbyshire DE 55 6HA. Tel: 01773 875105
Pitstop 90 (bike engines) – 96 Nottingham Road, Ripley, Debyshire DE5 3AX. Tel: 01773 512333. www.pitstop90.co.uk
Real Steel (V8s) – Unit 9, Tomo Industrial Estate, Packet Boat Lane, Cowley, Middlesex UB8 2JP. Tel: 01895 440505
Rover Breakers (K-series engines) – Tel: 01606 45911. www.roverbreakers.com
RPI Engineering (Rover V8) – Wayside Garage, Holt Road, Horsford, Norwich, Norfolk NR10 3EE. Tel: 01603 891209. wwwv8engines.com
Two To Four Engineering (bike engines) – Main Street, Sedgeberrow, Evesham, Worcestershire WR11 6UF. Tel: 01386 881283
Vulcan Engineering (largely Ford) – 185 Uxbridge Road, Hanwell, London W7 3TH. Tel: 0208-579 3202. www.vulcanengines.com

LOCOST COMPONENT SUPPLIERS

Kit Car & Locost Regalia – 17 Bowood Road, Old Town, Swindon, Wiltshire SN1 4LP. Tel: 01793 529031. www.kitcar-regalia.7p.com
Lolocost – Oxclose Lane, Mansfield Woodhouse, Notts NG19 8DF. Tel: 01623 422286. www.monospares.co.uk
Luego – Tel: 01487 815643. www.luegoracing.com
MK Engineering – Unit 10 Harrison Drive Industrial Estate, Langold, Worksop, Notts S81 9RL. Tel: 01909 731187. www.mkeenan.freeserve.co.uk
Nitron (dampers) – 2 Bampton Road, Black Bourton, Oxon OX18 2PD. Tel: 01993 844449
NR Engineering Services – 5 Robert Street, Thornaby, Cleveland TS17 6AN. Tel: 01642 863716
Stuart Taylor Motorsport – Unit 12 Pinfold Trading Estate, Pinfold Lane, Stapleford, Nottingham NG9 8DL. Tel: 01159 399497. www.stuart-taylor.co.uk
Triton Sports Cars – Tel: 01327 341577. www.locost7.co.uk

STAINLESS NUTS AND BOLTS

Aidpac – 16 Wilkinson Avenue, Bradley, Bilston WV14 8PS. Tel: 01902 560327. www.stainlessman.co.uk
Namrick – 124 Portland Road, Hove, Sussex BN3 5QL. Tel: 01273 779864

TRIMMING SUPPLIERS (CARPET, VYNIL ETC)

Creech Coachtrimming Centre – 45 Anerley Road, Crystal Palace, London SE19 2AS. Tel: 0208-659 4135. E-mail: creech.cc@ukgateway.net
DM Middleton – Unit D Middleton Business Park, Cartwright Street, Cleckheaton, West Yorks BD19 5LU. Tel: 01274 871509
Intatrim – Unit 1-2, Trench Lock 2, Telford, Shropshire TF1 4SW. Tel: 01952 641712
M&M Classic Car Components – Tel: 01775 640423
Martrim Coach Trimming & Supplies – Unit 9, King's Street Trading Estate, Middlewich, Cheshire CW10 9LM. Tel: 01606 834480
Woolies – Northfields Industrial Estate, Market Deeping, Peterborough PE6 8AR. Tel: 01778 347347. www.woolies-trim.co.uk

SHOCK ABSORBERS AND SPRINGS

AVO Motorsport – Caswell Road, Brackmills Ind. Est., Northampton, Northamptonshire NN4 7PL. Tel: 01604 708101. www.avouk.co.uk
Dampertech – Brampton Hall, Brampton Road, Brampton-En-Le-Morthen, Rotherham S66 9BD. Tel: 01709 703992

PROPSHAFT MODIFICATIONS/BALANCING

Autoprop – Tel: 01342 322623
Dunning & Fairbank Ltd – Cross Green Rise, Cross Green Approach, Leeds LS9 0SD. Tel: 0113 2488788. www.propshafts.co.uk
Reco-Prop – Unit 4, Newtown Trading Estate, Chase Street, Luton, Beds. LU1 3QZ. Tel: 01582 412110. www.reco-prop.com

PLUMBING (OIL, WATER ETC)

BGC Motorsport – 55 Lady's Drove, Emneth, Nr Wisbech, Cambs PE14 8DF. Tel: 01945 466690. www.bgcmotorsport.co.uk
Speedflow – Tel: 0208 530 6664. wwwspeedflow.co.uk

WIRING

Trust Electrical – Tel: 01904 608899
Premier Wiring Systems – Tel: 0800 0742789. www.premierwiring.co.uk
Vehicle Wiring Products (brochure) – 9 Buxton Court, Manners Industrial Estate, Ilkeston, Derbyshire DE7 8EF. Tel: 0115 9305454

INSTRUMENT SPECIALISTS

ETB Instruments – 17 Leighcliff Building, Maple Av., Leigh-on-sea, Essex SS9 1DJ. Tel: 01702 711127
Saturn Industries – 10-14 Newland Street, Coleford, Forest of Dean, Gloucestershire GL16 8AN. Tel: 01594 834321
Speedy Cables (instruments only) – Abercrave, Swansea, SA9 1SQ. Tel: 01639 732213
Speedy Cables (cables only) – Unit 14, Merchant Drive, Hertsford, Herts, SG13 7AZ. Tel: 01992 581600

EXHAUST SPECIALISTS

Custom Chrome – 37-38 Seymour Road, Nuneaton, Warks CV11 4JD. Tel: 024 76387808. www.custom-chrome.co.uk

JP Exhausts – Old School House, Brook Street, Macclesfield, Cheshire SK11 7AW. Tel: 01625 619916
Longlife Exhausts – 128 Stanley Park Road, Carshalton, Surrey SM5 3JG. Tel: 0208-669 1719. www.exhausts.uk.com

FIBREGLASS SUPPLIERS

CFS – 01209 822200
Corrosion Protection Systems – Tel: 0208 300 2800
Glassplies – 2 Crowland Street, Southport, Lancs PR9 7RL. Tel: 01704 540626

SEAT SUPPLIERS

Cobra Seats – Unit D1 and D2, Halesfield 23, Telford TF7 4NY. Tel: 01952 684020. www.cobraseats.com
Corbeau Seats – Unit 17, Wainwright Close, Churchfields Industrial Estate, St Leonards-on-Sea, E. Sussex TN38 9PP. Tel: 01424 854499. www.corbeau-seats.co.uk
Intatrim – Unit 1-2, Trench Lock 2, Telford, Shropshire TF1 4SW. Tel: 01952 641712

WHEEL SUPPLIERS

Compomotive – Components Automotive Ltd., Units 4,5,6 Wulfrun Trading Estate, Stafford Road, Wolverhampton, West Midlands WV10 6HG. Tel: 01902 311499. www.comp.co.uk
Eddie White Motorsport (Ford – large stock of second-hand) – 48 Evershill Lane, Morton, Alfreton, Derbyshire DE 55 6HA. Tel: 01773 875105
Elite Autos (general wheel and tyre supplier) – Unit A, Suttons Business Park, 136/138 New Road, Rainham, Essex RM13 8DE. Tel: 01708 525577. www.elitedirect.com
Image Wheels – Unit 3, Fountain Industrial Estate, Fountain Lane, Tipton, West Midlands DY4 9HA. Tel: 0121-522 2442. www.imagewheels.co.uk
Manx – Leisure Accessories, Brittania Works, Hurricane Way, Airport Industrial Estate, Norwich NR6 6EY. Tel: 01603 414551

WHEEL NUTS, BOLTS & SPACERS

Select Auto Supplies – 199 Duggins Lane, Tile Hill, Coventry CV4 9GP. Tel: 024 76465845

ALLOY WHEEL REFURBISHMENT

Spit and Polish – 12B, Sovereign Way, Tonbridge, Kent TN9 IRS. Tel: 01732 367771. www.spitandpolish.co.uk

GENERAL SUPPLIERS WITH FULL BROCHURE

Eddie White Motorsport (Free with 4x1st class stamps) – 48 Evershill Lane, Morton, Alfreton, Derbyshire DE55 6HA. Tel: 01773 875105
Europa Specialist Spares – Fauld Industrial Park, Tutbury, Burton-Upon-Trent, Staffordshire DE12 9HR. Tel: 01283 815609. www.europaspares.com
Holden Vintage & Classic Ltd – Linton Trading Estate, Bromyard, Herefordshire HR7 4QT. Tel: 01885 488000. www.holden.co.uk
Stafford Vehicle Components – Unit 53, Kepler, Off Mariner, Litchfield Road Industrial Estate, Tamworth, Staffs. B79 7SF. Tel: 01827 67714. www.s-v-c.co.uk

SPORTS ORIENTATED SUPPLIERS (OIL COOLERS, FANS)

Merlin Motorsport – Castle Combe Circuit, Chippenham, Wilts. SN14 7EX. Tel: 01249 782101. www.merlinmotorsport.co.uk

KIT BUILD-UP SPECIALISTS

Cadini Motorsport – Tel: 01202 894009. www.kitcarbuilders.co.uk
Roadtech – Hyders Farmhouse, Bonnetts Lane, Ifield, Crawley, West Sussex RH11 0NY. 01293 550808
Royle – The Old School, Staindrop, Darlington DL2 3NH. Tel: 01833 660452. www.david-royle.co.uk
SSC – Hillcrest, Tylwch Llandidloes, Powys SY18 6JR. Tel: 01686 413000. www.specialistsportscars.com
Thunderbird Racing – Tel: 01623 722288

INSURANCE SERVICES

Adrian Flux & Company – Tel: 0845 1303400
AW Marlow – Tel: 01283 740440
Cheshunt Insurance – Tel: 01992 643255
CIC Insurance – Tel: 01206 792927
Footman James & Co – Tel: 0121 561 4196
Graham Sykes Insurance – Tel: 01395 266621
Hill House Hammond – Tel: 01733 310899
Hoddesdon Insurance Consultants – Tel: 08451 212212
Osborne & Sons – Tel: 0208 388 6060
Snowball Insurance – 01922 686116

SECOND-HAND KIT CAR BUYERS/SELLERS

Barry Brace – Tel: 01702 231319. www.affordablekit-cars@fsnet.co.uk
Fisher Sportscars – Underlyn Industrial Estate, Underlyn Lane, Marden, Kent TN12 9BQ. Tel: 01622 832977
Hallmark Cars – (Cobras and Westfields) Tel: 0208 529 7474. www.hallmark-cars.com.
Kitcar Classics – 1 Howard Road, Reigate, Surrey RH2 7JE. Tel: 01737 225888. www.britishkitcars.co.uk
Northwood Kitcars – 01923 823681
Specialist Sportscar Centre – Crediton, Devon. Tel: 01363 773772
Sussex Kit Cars – Chiddingly Road, Horam, East Sussex TN21 0JJ. Tel: 01435 812706.
Uxbridge Kitcars – Tel: 01895 624554. www.uxbridgekitcars.co.uk

MISCELLANEOUS

FIRE EXTINGUISHERS

Eddie White Motorsport, 48 Evershill Lane, Morton, Alfreton, Derbyshire DE55 6HA. Tel: 01773 875105

GENERAL GARAGE TOOLS

Machine Mart. Tel: 01602 411200 for catalogue and to find nearest dealer

INSTRUMENT REFURBISHEMENT AND CABLE MODIFICATION

Speedy Cables (cables only) – Unit 14, Merchant Drive, Hertsford, Herts, SG13 7AZ. Tel: 01992 581600

RUBBERCOAT UNDERSEALANT

Carlife, Westbrook Works, 140 Thornton Road, Bradford BD1 2DX. Tel: 01943 870148

TIE WRAPS AND GENERAL FASTENINGS

Mr Fast'ner, Unit 6/12 Warwick House Industrial Park, Banbury Road, Southam, Warwickshire CV33 0PS. Tel: 01926 817207

WINDSCREEN MAKE-UP

Triplex Replacement Services, Main Road, Queenborough, Kent ME11 5BB. Tel: 01795 663311

Appendix D

Club Listing

This is not a comprehensive club listing. Instead, we've tried to highlight those clubs with cars which fall into our £5000 budget, either to build or buy second-hand. If you cannot get hold of any club listed here then contact the Which Kit? offices for an updated address/telephone number on 01737 222030.

MARQUE CLUBS

AVIATORS GUILD (Blackjack) – Geoff Ryall-Harvey, 14 Forrest Pines, Wrexham LL13 9GJ. Tel: 01244 318123

BLACKJACK AVION CLUB – 17 Beech Hey Lane, Willaston, South Wirrel CH64 1TS

BANHAM ENTHUSIASTS CLUB – Chris Hewson, 22 Keswick Close, Felixstowe IP11 9NZ

BOND OWNERS' CLUB – 42 Beaufort Avenue, Hodge Hill, Birmingham B34 6AE. Tel: 0121 784 4626

B.R.A. OWNERS CLUB – Dave Maddock, 26 Woodnoth Drive, Shavington, Crewe, Cheshire CW2 5BW. Tel: 01270 662176
Email: maddock@woodnoth.freeserve.co.uk

BURLINGTON OWNERS' CLUB – John Abbott, 112 Woolacombe Lodge Road, Selly Oak, Birmingham B29 6PY

CALVEY MITCHEL OWNERS' CLUB – Martin Scott, 7 Hazelwood, Benfleet, Essex SS7 4NW. Tel: 01268 750665

CARISMA OWNERS' CLUB – Ted Legg, 11 Olden Mead, Letchworth, herts SG6 2SP. Tel: 01462 673202

CLAN OWNERS' CLUB – James McEwan, 19 Greenacres, South Cornelly, Mid Glamorgan, CF33 4SE. Tel: 01332 767410

CLUB NOVA & AVANTE – Keith Stringer, 16A Dordon Road, Dordon, Tamworth, Staffs B78 1QN. Tel: 01827 705506.
Email: Keith.Stringer@ntlworld.com

CLUB ROTRAX – John Harding, 14 Chestnut Road, Sutton Benger, Chippenham, Wilts SN15 4RP. Tel: 01249 720494

CLUB STYLUS – Jeremy Bayne-Powell, Kimber Cottage, Glaziers Lane, Normandy, Guildford, Surrey GU3 2EB.

COVIN OWNERS' CLUB – AM Dykes, 7 Hazelcroft, Churchdown, Glos GL3 2DS. Tel: 01452 559951

DARIAN REGISTER – 4 Browns Lane, Uckfield, East Sussex TN22 1RS. Tel: 01825 763638

DASH SPORTSCAR CLUB – P. Barnes, 22 Agincourt Street, Heywood, Lancs OL10 3EY. Tel: 01706 624504

DAVRIAN REGISTER – 11-13 Gloucester Place, Briston, Melton Constable, Norfolk NR24 2LD. Tel: 01263 860525

DAX RUSH OWNERS' CLUB – Terry Roberts, Wylam Cottage, Beacon Close, Painswick, Stroud, Glos GL6 6UF

DOMINO CAR CLUB – Mark West, Porch Farm Cottage, Village Road, Coleshill, Bucks HP7 0LG. Tel: 01494 432074

DUTTON OWNERS' CLUB – Simon Dunn, 17 Oakcroft Road, Billesley, Birmingham B13 0HR. Tel: 0121 441 5070

EAGLE OWNERS' CLUB – Kerry & Lex Lockyer, 83 Old Bridge Road, Whitstable, Kent CT5 1RB

FORMULA 27 OWNERS' CLUB – Simon Laker, 14, Greys Road, Studley, Warwickshire B80 7QQ

FUGITIVE OWNERS' CLUB – John Dingley, 357 Clasemont Road, Morriston, Swansea, West Glamorgan SA6 6BU

GEMINI OWNERS' CLUB – Richard Adams, 4 Edgehill Road, Lighthorne Heath, Leamington Spa, Warwicks. Tel: 01926 311711

GENTRY REGISTER – Barbara Reynolds, Barn Close Cottage, Cromford Road, Woodlinkin, Derbyshire NG16 4HD. Tel: 01773 719874

GINETTA OWNERS' CLUB – Roger Bryson, 1 Furze Avenue, St. Albans, Herts AL4 9NQ

GTM OWNERS' CLUB – Terry Kenehan, 18 Slack Lane, Pilsley, Chesterfield, Derbyshire S45 8HH. Tel: 01773 875516.
E-mail: kenahan@clara.co.uk

JAGO OWNERS' CLUB – Chris Kilford, 44 Chatsworth Place, Meir, Stoke-on-Trent ST3 7DP. Tel: 01782 343691 (Daytime)

JBA OWNERS' CLUB – Les Fragle, Brock Cottage, 6 Thistleton Road, Thistleton, Preston, Lancs PR4 3XA. Tel: 01995 672230

JZR PILOTS' ASSOCIATION – Edgar Lowe, 130 Barrows Hill Lane, Westwood, Notts NG16 5HJ. Tel: 01773 810572

LOCUST ENTHUSIASTS' CLUB – Dave Gower, 101 Cleave Road, Gillingham, Kent ME7 4AT. Tel: 01634 230655.
E-mail: phil@q133kkl.freeserve.co.uk

LOCOST CAR CLUB – 1 Highfield Drive, Garforth, Leeds LS25 1JY.
E-mail: rory_perrett@lineone.net

LOMAX REGISTER – Peter Chitty, 8 Forest End, Courtmoor, Fleet, Hants GU13 9XE. Tel: 01252 620128

MARLIN OWNERS' CLUB – Mr D Nelson, 51 Queen Elizabeth Road, Frankley, Rubery, Birmingham B45 0NE Tel: 0121 453 7250

MIDAS OWNERS' CLUB – Tim Clark, 1 Grove End, Hilton, Huntingdon, Cambridgeshire PE28 9PF

MIDGE OWNERS & BUILDERS' CLUB – Dave Everall, 57 Wimberry Drive, Waterhayes, Newcastle Under Lyme, Staffs ST5 7SG.

MINARI REGISTER – Dave Smith, 59 Penhill Road, Bexley, Kent DA5 3EP. Tel: 0181 303 7110. E-mail: dasmith@cwcom.net

NG OWNERS' CLUB – Bob Preece, 41 Gayfere Road, Stoneleigh, Epsom, Surrey KT17 2JY. Tel: 020 8393 4661

ONYX OWNERS' CLUB – John Wilkinson, 1 Bayone Avenue, Springfield, Grimsby DN33 3LN. Tel: 01472 316597

PILGRIM CAR CLUB – Sean V. Godfrey, Events Co-Ordinator, 6 Sister Dora Ave, Burntwood, Staffs. WS7 9QD. Tel: 01543 670439
Email: Pilgrimbreed@aol.com

QUANTUM OWNERS' CLUB – Mr M Hughes, 148 Weston Road, Billericay, Essex CM12 9JH. Tel: 01277 623523

RICKMAN CARS OWNERS' CLUB – Alan Burgess, 10 Stoney Way, Tetney, Lincs DN36 5PG. Tel: 01472 816471

ROBIN HOOD OWNERS' CLUB – Ian Cairns, 1 Winnipeg Close, Stoke-on-Trent ST4 8UE

SCAMP OWNERS' CLUB – Debbie Williams, 8 Bustlers Rise, Duxford, Cambridgeshire CB2 4QU. Tel: 01223 834722

SPARTAN OWNERS' CLUB – Peter Brown, 31 Fenmow Avenue, Bucknall, Stoke-on-Trent ST2 9NE.
Tel: 07752 827447 (day) 01782 266451 (eves)

SYLVA REGISTER – Andy Wallis, 12A Eaton Place, Brighton BN2 1EH. Tel: 01273 607263

TEAL OWNERS' CLUB – Mike Birch, Cromer Mill, Cromer, Nr. Walkern, Stevenage, Herts SG2 7QE. Tel: 01763 281412

TEMPEST REGISTER – John Box, The Stables, Thornleigh Drive, Burton in Kendal, Carnforth, Lancs LA6 1NQ. Tel: 01524 781841

TIGER OWNERS' CLUB – Adam Wilkins, 57 London Road, Teynham, Kent ME9 9QW

TRIAD OWNERS' CLUB – Alan Dee, 100 Curborough Road, Lichfield, Staffs WS13 7NR. Tel: 01543 416107

UVA FUGITIVE OWNERS' CLUB – John Dingley, 357 Clasemount Road, Morriston, Swansea, West Glamorgan SA6 6BU

WESTFIELD SPORTS CAR CLUB – Mark Stanton, 102 Broadmoor Avenue, Smethwick, Warley, West Midlands B67 6JU

AREA CLUBS

BRISTOL CLASSIC, SPORTS & KIT CAR CLUB – Graham Best, 12 Hortham Lane, Almondsbury, Bristol BS12 4JH

CLEVELAND KIT CAR & SPECIALS OWNERS' CLUB – Ian Churns, 54 Bolckow Street, Guisborough, Cleveland TS14 6EN. Tel: 01287 209885. E-mail: ian.churns@dtn.btl.com

GRIMSBY KIT CAR CLUB – 89 Springfield Road, Grimsby, South Humberside DN33 3LG

HANTS & BERKS KIT CAR CLUB – Colin Jones, 3 Hillside Cottages, Frogmore, Camberley, Surrey

HERTS AND BEDS ALTERNATIVE CAR CLUB – T. Alvis, 21 Caslon Way, Letchworth, Herts SG6 4QJ. Tel: 01462 675092

KENT KIT CAR CLUB – Jenny Willett, 31 Bathurst Road, Staplehurst, Tonbridge, Kent TN12 0LG. Tel: 01580 892949

NORTH EAST KIT CAR CLUB – 11 Badmington Avenue, Boldon Colliery, Tyne & Wear NE35 9LD

NORTH WEST KIT CAR CLUB – Paul Crane, 17 Yarncroft, Tyldesley, Manchester M29 7PL. Tel: 01942 875166

NOTTINGHAMSHIRE KIT CAR CLUB – Steve Marley, 20 Hometield Avenue, Arnold, Nottingham NG5 8GA. Tel: 01602 2641/8

SCOTTISH KIT CAR CLUB – Jackie Grundy, 3 Laurel Place, Bonnybridge, Stirlingshire

SOUTH EAST FISHER/SYLVA REGISTER – Mac Allardyce, 9 Quested Way, Harrietsham, Maidstone, Kent ME17 1JG. Tel: 01622 859449

SOUTH WALES KIT CAR CLUB – Tom James, 17 Buckingham Place, Highlight Park, Barry, South Glamorgan CF62 8AT

SUFFOLK COASTAL KIT CAR CLUB – Tony Gould, 7 Harkstead Lane, Woolverstone, Ipswich, Suffolk IP9 1BB. Tel: 01473 780777

SUSSEX KIT CAR CLUB – Dave Bray, Chiddingly Road, Horam, Nr. Heathfield, East Sussex TN21 0JJ. Tel: 01435 812706

ULSTER KIT CAR CLUB – Stephen Traynor, 530 Antrim Road, Glengormley, Co, Antrim BT36 8DD. Tel: 01232 833686.

WESSEX KIT CAR CLUB – Chris Parrott, 64 Meadow Way, Verwood, Wimborne, Dorset BH31 6HG. Tel: 01202 825503

WEST CUMBRIA KIT CAR CLUB – Erica Postitenwaite, 11 Coniston Avenue, Seascale, Cumbria, CA20 1LP. Tel: 01946 728462

YORKSHIRE ALTERNATIVE CAR CLUB – Colin Tait, 24 Pinfold Lane, Methley, Leeds LS26 9AB. Tel: 01977 515360

GENERAL CLUBS

2CVGB – David Tilbey, 303 Yorktown Road, College Town, Sandhurst, Berks GU47 0QA

750 MOTOR CLUB – Robin Knight Tel: 01379 384268

CITROEN SPECIALS' CLUB – R D Lloyd, The Oaks, Preston, Gubbles Road, Bomeve Heath, Nr Shrewsbury SY4 3LU

CLASSIC CROSSBRED CLUB – Paul Robins, 43 Marischal Road, Lewisham, London SE13 5LE

ENTHUSIASTS' KIT CAR CLUB – K. Dodd, 26 Boulsey Rise, Ottershaw, Chertsey, Surrey KT16 0JX

FEDERATION OF KIT CAR CLUBS – Dave James, 31 Patrick Road, West Bridgford, Nottingham NG2 7QE

HISTORIC SPECIALS REGISTER – Richard Disbrow, 16 the Close, Blandford Forum, Dorset DT11 7HA. Tel: 01258 454879

MARCHES KIT CAR CLUB – Andy Smith, Event Organiser, 28 Stanberrow Road, Redhill, Hereford HR2 7NF

MONGRELS KIT CAR CLUB – Paul Davison, 9 Lydd Close, Lincoln LN6 0NZ. Tel: 01522 885748

NATIONAL BUGGY REGISTER – Mark Haynes, 26 Birkdale Drive, Alwoodley, Leeds LS17 7SZ. Tel: 01132 684310

NUTCRACKERS CAR GROUP – Heys Villa, The Heys, Coppull, Chorley, Lancs PR7 4NX. Tel: 01257 792387

POTTERIES KIT CAR CLUB – Stephen Myatt, 103 Chell Green Avenue, Chell, Stoke-on-Trent, Staffs ST6 7LA

Index

About the author	144
Accessory directory	138-139
Accessory stands	33
Alternative reading	144
Ancillary costs	28
Autotune Gemini	16, 79, 134
Axle stands	27
Blackjack Avion	41-48, 66
Body conversions	17
BRA	15, 131
Brochures	21
Budgeting	24
BWE Locust	130
Caterham Seven	13
Citroen 2CV	43
Club listing	140
Cobra replicas	11
Colour section	65-80
Contact details	136
Dakar	17, 135
Dax Camber Compensation	10
Dax Tojeiro	8
Deauvill Canard	77, 130
Dutton	7
Electrical hazards	27
Eye protection	27
Factory visits	23
Falcon LX3	78, 131
Fans	31
Fereday Vario	133
Fiat twin-cam	36
Fiero Factory Euro 427	11
Fire hazards	27
Fisher Fury	6, 56-62, 68
Ford Pinto	53
Ford X-flow	36, 59, 62, 100
Ford Zetec	13, 36, 58
Formula 27	13, 129
Free Spirit	78, 132
Fuse boxes	33
Gear knobs	32
Grinnall Scorpion	16
GT Buggy	21, 135
GTM Libra Spyder	41
GTM Libra	9
Honda Fireblade	54, 60
Instruments	31, 32
Insurance	26
Jaguar V12	81
JAS Buggy	17, 70-71, 88-94
JBA Falcon	15
JZR	132
Kawasaki ZX9	37
Kit car types	11-18
Leighton	132
Lighting	26
Locost	29, 95-102
Locust	29
Lomax	15, 78, 131
Lotus 7 inspired replicas	12
Marlin Sportster	15, 78, 130
Midas Gold Conv.	16, 79, 134
Mirage	21
Mirrors	31, 32
MK Indy	49-55, 67, 72
NCF Blitz	80, 133
Nostalgia XK120	14
Nova	41
Onyx Bobcat	80, 133
Owners' clubs	23
Paul Banham	14, 73, 103-111, 79, 134, 135
Pembleton	132
Reducing costs	29-33
Replicas	14
Robin Hood	8, 63-64, 69, 81-82
Rover V8	58
RV Dynamics Bugrat	133
Safety issues	27
Scamp	133
Scrap yards	30
Seat runners	32
Seats	32
Setting up costs	26
Show dates	137
Side indicators	30, 33
Sliding pillar suspension	86
Sports Cars	16
Stuart Taylor	12, 77, 129
SVA	28
Switches	31, 32
Sylva Striker	12, 75-76, 119-128
Tempest	74, 112-118
Three-wheelers	15
Tiger	12, 34-40, 65
Tools	26
Traditional tourers	14
Tri-Tech	132
Vindicator	77, 130, 134
Visiting shows	22
VW Beetle	17, 18
YKC Pace	133

About the Author

A career in agriculture went to seed as soon as Ian Stent found out he could build a replica of the AC Cobra in his garage for a fraction of the price of the real thing. Despite failing to secure his dream car, he joined *Which Kit?* magazine in 1990 and hasn't looked back since, becoming editor in 1993 and remaining at the helm until going freelance in 1998. Still heavily involved with the magazine and kit cars in general, he now writes for a number of other automotive titles, including *Mini World* and *Car Import Guide*.

Over the years Ian has built a number of kit cars himself and overseen the assembly of many in-house build projects. He currently runs a CC Cyclone and has recently taken on the restoration of a GTM Coupe. He has also been involved in the writing and production of a number of kit car books, including *The Which Kit? Guide To Kit Car Building* and *Performance Roadsters*, although this is the first book to have been completely written by him.

Other books available from the publisher include:

THE COMPLETE GUIDE TO KIT CARS, 2002/2003 – Every last kit car, famous or obscure, notorious or naughty, fabulous or ferocious, is covered in this comphrehensive, high quality publication. UK price: £7.50 inc p&p.

THREE-WHEELERS – Here's the complete story of trikes, from 1885 right up to the current day. With over 160 pages and 300 photographs, it is surely the most comprehensive book ever compiled on this barmy scene. UK price: £18 inc p&p.

HOW TO BUILD A KIT CAR – Dealing with everything from initial factory visits and choosing your kit, right through to final registration once the car is complete, you won't find a more comprehensive book of the art of building kit cars. UK price: £20 inc p&p.

THE WHICH KIT? GUIDE – This annually updated publication is a great introduction to the kit car industry. All the major manufacturers are listed, along with details of the donor cars required, kit contents, budget on-the-road costs and current addresses and brochure prices etc. UK price: contact Blueprint Books on 01737 222030 for more information.

KIT CAR ELECTRICS – Part of the *Car Builder's Handbook* series. This is one of the most daunting areas of a kit car build for many enthusiasts. *Kit Car Electrics* guides you through the various different areas of a kit car's wiring, with clear and concise information, pictures and diagrams. UK price: £11.95 inc p&p.

REBUILDING AND TUNING FORD X-FLOW AND PINTO ENGINES – Part of the *Car Builder's Handbook* series. A hands-on, practical guide to engine building and tuning for the amateur enthusiast, including basic gas-flowing, tuning principles, converting to a 5-speed gearbox and sorting ignition problems. UK price: £15.95 inc p&p.

CLASSIC KIT CARS – The ultimate reference for enthusiasts of all kit cars built between 1953 and 1985. An exhaustive listing giving details on production numbers, good and bad points to buying second-hand and contact details for any cars still in production. Photographs of every car outlined. The bible for kit car enthusiasts everywhere. UK price: £15 inc p&p

To make a credit card order or for a comprehensive listing of other motoring books available from the publisher, please contact: **Autocraft Publications, 1 Howard Road, Reigate, Surrey RH2 7JE. Tel: 01737 222030.**